In this volume Miss Anthony creates a new type of biography by doing for her central figure what the modern novelist does for the heroine of his story. It is not a chronicle of facts, dates, and books, but a searching psychological study of the inner motives that made Margaret Fuller our first professional woman of letters, and the first American feminist. Miss Anthony does the same thing, incidentally, for some of Margaret Fuller's friends, Emerson, Greeley, and Carlyle, giving, for example, in a page or two, the very heart of Carlyle's tragedy.

MARGARET FULLER

From the *Century Magazine*, April, 1893

MARGARET FULLER

A PSYCHOLOGICAL BIOGRAPHY

BY

KATHARINE ANTHONY

AUTHOR OF "MOTHERS WHO MUST EARN," "FEMINISM
IN GERMANY AND SCANDINAVIA"

NEW YORK
HARCOURT, BRACE AND COMPANY
1921

PREFACE

THE life of Margaret Fuller has been the happy hunting-ground of imaginative biographers. The Bacchante, the Sybil, the Pythoness,—these were the usual clarifying terms in which she was explained to the generations which succeeded her. After this Margaret myth had been current for more than thirty years, Mr. Thomas Wentworth Higginson sought to inject some realism into the picture. In his excellent biography, he politely denounced the romantic legend and represented Margaret as the woman of action which she really was. But he was chiefly concerned with the literary pioneer, and Margaret was, after all, more interesting as a personality than as a writer. About the same time, Mrs. Julia Ward Howe composed another life, emphasizing Margaret's pioneer work for the emancipation of women and also eliminating the "Pythian disguise," the "viraginian aspect," and all the rest of the inflamed rhetoric which had contributed so largely to Margaret's previous reputation. But Mrs. Howe was so magnificently impersonal, that she leaves us more in the dark than ever as to what manner of woman this really was who was so startling and upsetting to her own generation. Finally, Margaret's *Love Letters* were published, scrupulously edited and pruned by one knows not how many censors. A realistic interpretation of her life and character has not only not been attempted but has rather been positively avoided. A mood of evasion has marked almost all that has been written about her. The following study tries to arrive at the realities of Margaret's personality and career, chiefly by means of modern psychological analysis.

My purpose has been to apply a new method to old matter. I have not tried to unearth fresh material or discover unpublished evidence. The sources from which the facts are drawn are well-known volumes given in the bibliography at the end. But the following pages are less concerned with a chronology of facts than with the phases of a complex personality and a manifold life. It is an attempt to analyze the emotional values of an individual existence, the motivation of a career, the social transformation of a woman's energies.

In order to give direct representation, Margaret's writings are liberally quoted. Her books are now forgotten and neglected, the only editions in existence being so out of date that few libraries are old enough to possess them. Yet she wrote much good criticism, good feminism, and good psychology, which deserve to be rescued from the dusty attic and classed with some of our newest wisdom.

Many circumstances combine to lend a special interest to Margaret Fuller at this time. Seventy years ago, she stood at the beginning of two great movements which have reached their culmination in our day. She saw the inception of the woman movement in America and the revolutionary movement in Europe. Her life, with all its inward and outward struggles, was peculiarly identified with both. Her ideals have recently renewed their vitality for us. For instance, now that suffrage is out of the way, there is a great need for the broader kind of feminism that Margaret Fuller represented. And, similarly, her relation to the European crisis of 1848 gives her also a relation to the second chapter of those revolutionary processes through which we are living today.

In short, Margaret was a modern woman who died in 1850. The legend she left cannot be truth. It was created mainly by unemancipated men; Chivalry and Puritanism combined to distort the picture. For this reason, her life demands a vindication from certain quarters which too long have failed her. *Feminisme oblige.* Her story needed to be told by some one who could sympathize with her struggles and affirm her ideals. Therefore, while striving for realism and impartiality, the following study does not pretend to avoid the warmth of the advocate.

K. A.

CONTENTS

MARGARET FULLER

CHAPTER I

FAMILY PATTERNS

MARGARET FULLER'S father was thirty-two when she was born. A self-made man, he had been compelled to postpone marriage and family life until a comparatively advanced age. But it was written that in the springtime of his thirty-first year, the Puritan lawyer and politician should succumb to his first romance. Less than a year later—on May 23, 1810— he became the father of a daughter.

It was almost an incidental fact that the young wife, who had married a man fully ten years older than herself, became a mother at the same time, for she proved to be the merest footnote of a mother. Her influence appears to have been limited to the physical acts of motherhood and to have terminated with her daughter's very brief term of infancy. The house in Cambridge and the second-story chamber in which she was brought to bed of Margaret are still shown to visitors; and one can almost imagine Timothy Fuller in the pangs of a *couvade* in the adjoining chamber. But if his jealousy of the maternal adventure did not carry him thus far, it stepped in at the earliest possible moment that nature would permit. He took the child's life in hand with a thoroughness which amounted to a practical kidnaping from the mother, and taught her to cleave only to him.   To celebrate his daughter's birth, he planted two elms in front of his house, and as they flourished and grew they typified the strong emotional bond which grew up between father and daughter in spite of more than thirty intervening years.

Margaret likened this relationship to that between Prospero and Miranda.   In her *Woman in the Nineteenth Century,* she described it thus: " [Miranda's] father was a man who cherished no sentimental reverence for Woman, but a firm belief in the equality of the sexes.   She was his eldest child, and came to him at an age when he needed a companion.   From the time she could speak and go alone, he addressed her not as a plaything, but as a living mind. Among the few verses he ever wrote was a copy addressed to his child, when the first locks were cut from her head. . . . He respected his child, however, too much to be an indulgent parent. . . . In so far as he possessed the keys to the wonders of this universe, he allowed free use of them to her, and, by the incentive of a high expectation, he forbade . . . that she should let the privilege lie idle."

There is in Mount Auburn a solid, four-square monument which sets forth the sum of Timothy Fuller's political achievements. It states that he graduated at Harvard University in 1801; was a member of the Massachusetts Senate from 1813 to 1816; a representative in the United States Congress from 1817 to 1825; speaker of the Massachusetts House of Representatives in 1825; and a member of the Executive Council in 1828. He was, in fact, a man of some distinction, and, in his little daughter's eyes, every inch a Roman Senator. According to his tombstone, Mr. Fuller adjusted successfully to the society into which he was born. He had a caustic tongue, liked to stand with the opposition in politics, and, notwithstanding his election successes, was not a " good mixer." It was true, as Margaret said, that he needed a companion.

Some years after her father's death, Margaret, after spending an afternoon at Mount Auburn, went home and wrote this note in her Journal: " Reasons why there are no good monuments? I must write upon this subject." To this she added another reflection, " Persons die generally, not as a natural thing, but from extraneous causes." But she was not thinking of old age as the natural cause of death.—" A death from love would be perfectly natural," she concluded. From girlhood Margaret betrayed a great deal of this kind of insight which nowadays goes by the name of Freudian psychology.

The Fullers sprang from the Puritan ghetto of Salem. The first Fuller was a blacksmith who experienced a passionate conversion under the preaching of the "soul-ravishing Mr. Shepherd." This pious ancestor was a contemporary of the Salem witches and one of the founders of the church in which witch "investigations" of those days were held. Fortunately, none of the female Fullers of that generation were witches. Margaret was the first of the clan to achieve this melancholy distinction.

Another strongly marked figure in Margaret's gallery of ancestors was a certain Timothy Fuller of Salem, called "Old Tim," who was the hero of a peculiar legend. Working in the fields one day, he grew thirsty and called at a house for a drink. The woman, who was just putting her baby to sleep, replied, "you rock the cradle while I draw the cider." On her return, the stranger asked her jocularly for the child in the cradle and the woman told him he must wait eighteen years. To this stipulation the suitor agreed, and, at the appointed time, returned and married the eighteen-year-old girl. Whether the legend is true or not, it suggests a parallel to what actually happened to Margaret Fuller who began to be a companion to her father while still an infant in the cradle.

Margaret's grandfather was a clergyman in Princeton, Massachusetts, when the Revolutionary War broke out. Whether he was pro-British or pacifist does not appear, but at any rate he preached a sermon on the text: " Let not him that girdeth on the harness boast himself as he that putteth it off,"—and was promptly discharged by his congregation, which consisted largely of minute-men. He sued the town for his salary, with the result that he was doubly dismissed and had moreover to pay the costs of the legal proceedings. In the end, the unfrocked but still unbeaten clergyman settled on a farm in the vicinity and got himself elected to the constitutional convention. His five sons, with one accord, forsook the ministry and took to the law.

Timothy Fuller and his four brothers put themselves through Harvard College in spite of narrow means and harsh obstacles. They were the kind of young men of whom it was proudly said by a descendant that they " grudged the hours that nature demands for sleep." True Puritans as they were, they regarded nature generally with a most begrudging eye and reveled in the dark worship of hardship for hardship's sake. There was an Uncle Abraham who remained a bachelor all his days and who presumed to teach Thomas Wentworth Higginson's mother how to darn better than she had ever darned before. Higginson says this shows how arrogant and self-assertive Uncle Abraham was,—this being a trait of the Fuller clan which Margaret inherited. But it shows something else, and that is that Uncle Abraham could darn. So could Margaret's father, Congressman Timothy Fuller; for he not only instructed his daughter in the classics but he guided her training in the domestic arts as well. Her dress, her correspondence, her parties—all this fell under the paternal supervision. Again one has to comment that such efficiency in a Congressman argues a feminine disposition rather than the reverse. Margaret must have imbibed in early childhood the idea that occupations were not divinely ordained for each sex. If father and Uncle Abraham could darn, why should she not go to sea? And so it came about that Margaret, having been brought up by hand by a father who had certain so-called feminine traits, became a woman who had certain so-called masculine traits. Such men and women confound the categories and are usually unpopular.

Margaret's father, the eldest of the Fuller brothers, was a non-conformist in religion and politics, being a Unitarian and a Jeffersonian. In those days, this was to be an unbeliever and a Jacobin. While still in college, he began his career of non-conformity. As a poor parson's son, obliged to work his way through college, he took part in a students' rebellion organized against certain hated regulations. For this indiscretion he lost his chance of being first-honor man and graduated with second honors instead. It was also while he was still in college that he became a disciple of Jefferson, who—as one critic said—" wrote such stuff about the will of the majorities as a New Englander would lose his rank among men of sense to avow." Nevertheless Timothy Fuller must needs avow them in the face of the fact that all the wealth and business of Boston were solidly on the other side. As the father of a large family his course was imprudent and led him at last almost into bankruptcy.

But Margaret had little appreciation of the complexities in her father's character, which were to so great an extent repeated in her own. She thought her father was a good business man. " He was a man largely endowed with that sagacious energy, which the state of New England society, for the last half century, has been so well fitted to develop. . . . As a boy, my father was taught to think only of preparing himself for Harvard University, and when there of preparing himself for the profession of the law. . . . The result was a character, in its social aspect, of quite the common sort. A good son and brother, a kind neighbor, an active man of business . . . he was but one of a class, which surrounding conditions have made the majority among us." But all this was only one side of the eccentric man, who enjoyed music with passionate delight, played the flute with some skill, and fell in love at first sight with a handsome girl who was worse than penniless, for she was well-endowed with poor relations. This last was not the act of a sagacious man of business.

"In the more delicate and individual relations," wrote Margaret, " he never approached but two mortals, my mother and myself." A man of few relationships, he naturally inclined towards intensity in those which he did form. In politics his name was frequently associated with that of John Quincy Adams, towards whom Fuller displayed an unfaltering and loyal friendship. He worked indefatigably in Adams's campaign for the presidency and in the summer of 1826 gave a great party for his chief at his home in Cambridge. Such a party had not been given in Cambridge for fifty years, and what a strain it must have been on the frugal household of the Fullers! Of course it gave the family the proud status of having entertained the President and helped to vindicate the social position of the Timothy Fullers in the eyes of the Federalist aristocracy of Boston. But it was apparently a sentimental party, after all,—an outburst of affection on the part of the over-reserved Mr. Fuller. At any rate, it netted him nothing in a business way, for it was not so long after this that his law practice entered its last fatal decline.

Having married so late, the poor man was caught by middle age with a large family of young children. When he was fifty the family baby was but two years old. He kept up the struggle for five years longer, and then decided to abandon Boston and retire with his large family to a farm—as his father had done before him. Margaret, who was but twenty-three, thought his retreat was ignoble. She " secretly wondered how a mind which had, for thirty years, been so widely engaged in the affairs of men, could care so much for trees and crops." Nevertheless, she went with the family to the farm and was more of a companion to her father than ever. He varied his occupation as a farmer with writing a history of the United States, and Margaret shared in the reading for this. But she hated the farm and there was now something inimical in her " companionship." The broken man lived but two years longer and then succumbed to the Asiatic cholera.

Through all this, Mrs. Fuller seems to have been the perfect example of the self-effacing mother. She had nine children in sixteen years, and was commemorated on her tombstone as " a true woman." One of her sons said of her : " Duty was her daily food. Self-sacrifice was as natural to her as self-

gratification is to others". When the Fullers had
guests, Mr. Fuller and his daughter entertained
them, while Mrs. Fuller merely appeared as a shy
and awkward figure in the background. In brief,
Margaret had crowded her mother out of her right-
ful position in the family with the most complete
success. It was no wonder that she grew up so bold,
and, as she herself said, "at nineteen the most intolerable girl that ever took a seat in a drawing-room."
If Mrs. Fuller had not been such a true and self-
sacrificing woman, her oldest daughter would have
had better manners. But she seems to have yielded
her place to her daughter without a protest, consoling
herself with reminiscences of her prowess as a school-
mistress before her marriage. She brought up her
younger children on the story of how she had once
soundly feruled a big boy who had questioned her
authority. But there is no indication that she ever
displayed such energy and courage in her own home.
She was a weak submissive woman, like the mother
of Mary Wollstonecraft. Perhaps there was a common reason why the daughters of both these mothers
have come down in history as aggressive women.

CHAPTER II

A PRECOCIOUS CHILD

INTELLECTUALLY and emotionally, Margaret Fuller was a precocious child. She had a hungry intellect and hungry emotions. When, as a mature woman, she visited Carlyle, his comment on her personality was: " Such a predetermination to eat this big Universe as her oyster or her egg, . . . I have not before seen in any human soul." Though Margaret was then thirty-six, her soul was still uncouth with hunger, like a voracious birdling in a nest, all wide-open beak and nothing else. She was lacking in the ingratiating marks of all the partial satisfactions which should have been her daily bread from childhood on. It was her tragedy that things came to her either too soon or too late: the essence of her fate was untimeliness.

Like her father and her grandfather, Margaret Fuller was educated at home, her school life away from home being practically negligible. She must have had a little domestic Harvard of her own, for her father had been a second-honor man and his father before him had been a second-honor man, so that Margaret's curriculum doubtless carried out the best

Harvard tradition. "My father was a man of business," she said, "even in literature."

Probably because his own education had been retarded by lack of means, Timothy Fuller was resolved to give his daughter an early start. At the age of six, she was taught Latin and English grammar, and read Latin daily from this time on. In translating, she was required to proceed "without breaks or hesitation,—for with these my father had absolutely no patience." A year or two later, she read Horace and Ovid, and before she reached her teens, she had learned to read French. "The great amount of study exacted of me soon ceased to be a burden, and reading became a habit and passion." At the age of eight, she read Shakespeare, Cervantes, and Molière. When she was twenty-five Emerson said of her that her reading was at a rate like Gibbon's.

There was no library in the Cambridgeport house, but her father had in his room a large closet filled with books. Here Margaret found the best writers of the eighteenth century,—the English novelists and the French political philosophers, in whose writings her father, who was "more than half a Jacobin," was especially well read. The priggish maiden read the French Republicans, but she did not like "Smollett, Fielding, and the like," because they dealt "too broadly with the coarse actualities of life."

Much has been made of Margaret's precocious studies as the cause of her life-long ill health. Margaret herself believed that the forcing of her intellect in tender years was the cause of her physical weakness and suffering, and her biographers have accepted her theory without criticism. Mrs. Howe thought that Margaret had a real case against her father; but, as a mother herself, she is reminded that there are "difficulties which parents encounter in the training of their children, and especially in that of their eldest-born," and she thought Margaret should not have criticized her well-intentioned parent. But Mr. Higginson pointed out that there was nothing peculiar about Margaret's education for that period, except that it was given to a girl. She was overtasked by her father merely because he trained her like a boy. If she *had been* a boy, she would not have been overtasked. "Cambridge boys, if the sons of college-bred men, were brought up in much the same way," says Higginson. Henry Hedge, who was Margaret's intimate friend and fellow-student, was ready for college at eleven, and had read as much Latin as she. Margaret must have been aware of young Hedge's attainments and she must have been aware, since they studied so much together, that her powers were on a par with his. Still, she had to find some theory for the miseries of her youth, and so she attributed her sufferings to over-study. But the truth was that, if Margaret had not been endowed with superior intelligence, all her father's efforts could not have stretched her mind to the span of such performances as he required of her. To this extent no violent hand was laid on her development.

But the by-products of Mr. Fuller's course were unwholesome. Margaret had to recite her lessons in the evening by candlelight, after her father's office hours were over. Thus the excitable child went to evening school and kept grown-up hours. If Mr. Fuller was interrupted, her bed-time was postponed to make up for it. And since he begrudged the hours that nature requires for sleep, apparently he begrudged them as well on Margaret's behalf. But it is doubtful whether these things alone would have shattered her health. Her vulnerable spot was her emotional precocity.

All her affections were focused on her father. He not only usurped the mother's place in addition to his own, but added to this the influence of the schoolmaster. In this triple character, he ruled his daughter's life completely, and she worshiped a trinity of authorities in him. Margaret's adult writings are full of echoes of her hectic, unchildish preoccupation with this attachment. "When I recollect how deep the anguish, how deeper still the want, with which I walked alone in hours of childish passion and called for a Father, after saying the word a hundred times, till it was stifled by sobs, how great seems the duty that name imposes." One would think that even a literary biographer would realize the uncanny eroticism of this reminiscence.

With characteristic candor, Margaret traces the emotional history of her childhood in a fragment of autobiography written at the age of thirty. It was based on an earlier history written at sixteen which she destroyed. Her record, brief as it is, contains almost a clinical picture of the future hysteric.

For the first five years of her life, Margaret enjoyed the position of an only child. During this time a baby sister made her appearance but she soon vanished again. " My earliest recollection is of a death," Margaret writes; " the death of a sister, two years younger than myself." She does not recall any feelings of tenderness towards this baby sister, but she thinks that " probably there is a sense of childish endearments such as belong to this tie." But she remembers vividly the funeral,—" the house all still and dark,—the people in their black clothes and dreary faces,—the scent of the newly-made coffin,—my being set up in a chair and detained by a gentle hand to hear the clergyman,—the carriages slowly going,—the procession slowly doling out their steps to the grave."

The reminiscence then proceeds rather more briskly: " My father,—all whose feelings were now concentered on me,—instructed me himself."

When Margaret was five, a baby brother was born. This was in the year 1815, and Mr. Fuller showed where his political sympathies lay by naming his infant son " Eugene." He delivered a Fourth of July oration at Watertown in his most caustic manner. " The ' disinterested and magnanimous Allies,' the ' deliverers of the world ', seem very *affectionate* to the world they have delivered. Their ' labor of love ' is only begun. One takes Poland under his gracious protection; another is pleased to take Norway; a third, Italy; and modest England resigns to each his favorite portion of prostrate Europe, and only claims, as a small gratuity, the rest of the world! " In this strain, the Honorable Timothy reviewed the events of 1815, at home as well as abroad no doubt, and his five-year-old daughter received a lasting imprint from the paternal view of things. From this time forth, we may always know where to find her.

In the picture of her childhood, Margaret pays great attention to her dreams. As a woman of thirty, she still recalls the child's dreams with great vividness. They haunted her all her life long, and she believed that, in some undefined way, they were the cause of her unhappiness. She did not know, however, that they furnished the key to the passionate conflicts from which she suffered. "These dreams," she says, writing of herself in the third person, "softened her heart too much, and cast a deep shadow over her young days; for then, and later, the life of dreams, —probably because there was in it less to distract the mind from its own earnestness,—has often seemed to her more real, and been remembered with more interest, than that of waking hours."

There was one dream which came to her repeatedly. "Often she dreamed of following to the grave the body of her mother, as she had done that of her sister, and wake to find the pillow drenched in tears." In this good child's heart, as in all good children's hearts, there were evil wishes which she had to keep secret even from herself. She had a primeval and murderous wish to attend the funeral of her beloved mother. But that is only half the story. The tears which wet her pillow were sincere, for the child also loved the gentle mother who was all self-effacing kindness. It was in the intensity of such early emotional conflicts that the foundation was laid for Margaret's neurotic disposition. The middle-aged Puritan father, who wished to renew his youth by spiritual loot from the next generation, was himself to blame for much of her suffering.

After her evening lessons, Margaret says that she went to bed with "nerves unnaturally stimulated,"

origin of life. "I remembered how, a little child,"
she says, "I had stopped myself one day on the stairs,
and asked, how came I here? How is it that I seem
to be this Margaret Fuller? What does it mean?
What shall I do about it?" In this sort of childish
inquiry was laid the foundation of her passion for
knowledge; she had a consuming wish to know and
understand the world. Ignorance was to her, she said,
"a pain."

A child like Margaret Fuller, of course, has day-
dreams as well as night dreams. Far back in the
"dewy dawn of memory," Margaret had thought of
herself as a "changeling" and pitied herself in her
"adopted home." Her real parents could not be this
commonplace New England couple whose thoughts
never strayed from the jobs of the day; she was a
European Princess confided to their care, and so forth.

She prayed earnestly for a sign,—"that it would
lighten in some particular region of the heavens, or
that I might find a bunch of grapes in the path when
I went forth in the morning. But no sign was
given, and I was left a waif stranded upon the shores
of modern life!" Children with intense imaginations
commonly have these superstitious fancies about their
magnificent origin and their power over impossibilities
by wishing. In Margaret the delusional life was
over-developed, but there are none so normal that they

can afford to smile at her childish absurdities from too
lofty a height.   Yet Emerson, who wished to prove
that Margaret had a "mountainous me," seriously
produced the fantasies of omnipotence from her early
childhood as evidence.   In order to show that " from
the beginning of her life she idealized herself as a
sovereign," he refers to a passage in her diary which
shows nothing of the kind, though it does show clearly
what an unhealthy emotional relationship existed between the Puritan child and her father.   " I remembered our walking in the garden avenue, between the
tall white lilies and Ellen's apple-tree; she was a
lovely child then, and happy, but my heart ached, and
I lived in just the way I do now.   Father said,
seeing me at a distance, ' *Incedo regina,*' etc.   Poor
Juno!   Father admired me, and, though he caused
me so much suffering, had a true sense at times of
what is tragic for me."   The chief peculiarity of
Margaret Fuller is that she remembered her childish
day-dreams and set them down so accurately.   Her
reminiscences are a distinct contribution to the psychology of normal childhood and it was only in the over-
accentuation of her emotions that they assumed a
neurotic coloring.

Margaret was clever enough to analyze the chief
injury of precocious learning in her own case.   Out
of her own experience, she laid down a principle which

modern educators are coming more and more to recognize. Her conclusion was that children should not learn to read too early, because "they should not through books antedate their actual experiences, but should take them gradually, as sympathy and interpretation are needed." As a result of her premature studies, her world was a world of demi-gods and Cæsars and the denizens of Cambridgeport did not shine by comparison. "How poor the scene around, how tame one's own existence, how meager and faint every power, with these beings in my mind! Often I must cast them quite aside in order to grow in my small way, and not sink into despair." Books should be to children, she thought, the aftermath, and not the vestibule, of experience. And they should be the same thing to an adult. "A moment of action in one's self," she said, "is worth an age of apprehension through others; not that our deeds are better, but that they produce a renewal of our being." Here again Margaret has laid down a principle of modern psychology. There are few better statements of the innate fertility of life and action as compared with the sterile pleasures of the day-dreamer's lot.

Margaret's neurotic childhood has always been a stumbling stone for her literary biographers. They were fascinated by it—indeed it seems for some of them to have been her chief attraction—but none of them has known what to make of it. Even Emerson, who detested that aspect of her nature, could not possibly pass it by. He shared the opinion of the Boston conclave that her hysterical sufferings were in some inexplicable way associated with her talents. Mrs. Howe speaks of the child's hysteria as if it were something afflicting but extraneous, like measles or scarlet fever. Kind Mr. Higginson, very much alive to the mischief which had been done to Margaret's reputation by dwelling on all this " seeress " and "arcana " business, strove to do justice to the commonplace and practical side of Margaret's life and character which has been so misrepresented. A gentleman of the old school, he thought there was something not altogether " nice " about hysteria, and so he left it out. McPhail, who put her life into his *Essays on Puritanism* where she most certainly belonged, had the good sense to compassionate suffering when he saw it and not to alternate between admiration and dislike. It was he who said also with sensible finality, that the child's character had puzzled and misled her biographers and would certainly continue to do so " till the essential nature of hysteria is disclosed."

So far as Margaret's case is concerned, Sigmund Freud's theory of hysteria is a perfect fit. As one of the Freudians has said, " It may be more comfortable to believe that hysteria is due to a toxic process than that it is due to psycho-sexual conflicts," but we shall have to make ourselves uncomfortable for the moment in the interests of the truth about Margaret Fuller's childhood. But how can an innocent child be the victim of a psycho-sexual conflict, some one protests. "The passions are not unfrequently felt in their full shock, if not in their intensity, at eight or nine years old." This is not a statement of those profoundly irritating Freudians but of Margaret Fuller herself, who wrote it in a book review in 1846. She frequently wrote the most surprising statements about the love-impulse which showed that she had more than an inkling of the truth about its nature and its history.

Margaret's whole emotional life in childhood centered around the father who likened her to Juno and wrote verses to a lock of her hair. In spite of the strictness of his Puritan régime, she knew herself to be the center of his attentions and his hopes. Some one suggested that Mr. Fuller educated his daughter to satisfy a social ambition. But to teach a girl Latin and send her into libraries in those days was the surest way of all to wreck her social prospects and dedicate her to spinsterhood. Mr. Fuller must have known that himself. Margaret said that her father educated her at home instead of sending her to school " merely to please himself." Evidently people thought that Mr. Fuller's motive for taking so much pains with his daughter needed an explanation. "He took pride in her precocious abilities, and enjoyed her companionship in his favorite studies," said Higginson; "that tells the whole story." It does, almost,—but not quite. The tie between father and daughter is never without some tinge of sex-attraction, and in the over-stressing of that tie lies the possibility of much neurotic suffering. In Margaret's case, without doubt, this early and natural affection was forced by the circumstances of her home-life into a premature strength and intensity. It became an *amour* which the sensitive consciousness was forced to drive down into the deepest and most secret recesses of its abandoned memories. Such impressions normally fade away with children and leave only their traces upon after-life; but with Margaret it was not so. Her childish love was the mainspring of her whole career

It stamped her with an unforgettable longing. As a woman of more than thirty, she walked along the seashore one day and saw a fisherman playing with his little girl. It struck her as a romantic idyll and she described it in these terms. "As I approached, I beheld a young fisherman with his little girl. He had nestled her into a hollow of the rock, and was standing before her, with his arms around her, and looking up in her face. Never was anything so pretty. I stood and stared, country fashion; and presently he scrambled up to the very top with her in his arms. She screamed a little as they went, but when they were fairly upon the crest of the rock, she chuckled and stretched out her tiny hand over his neck, to go still further. Yet, when she found he did not wish it, she leaned against his shoulder, and he sat feeling himself in the child like that exquisite madonna, and looking out over the great sea."

All this was merely a tender reminiscence out of Margaret's own childhood. Her rather bizarre picture of the man feeling himself in the child like a madonna was a fair portrait of the reserved, rather feminine, and affectionate father who did so much to make her what she was.

CHAPTER III

NARCISSA

AT the age of thirteen, Margaret fell violently in love. She fell in love " at first sight " (her life-long pattern for this process) with a stranger, whom she saw at church. The stranger was an English lady, who played the harp and read Sir Walter Scott. It was a sentimental and passing attachment, not a profound and life-long influence like Mary Wollstonecraft's for Fanny Blood. Margaret replaced the adored one from time to time by other matrons equally adored, but the original impression was never effaced.

All her pent-up feelings seized upon the strange lady as a drowning man clutches at a straw. " It was my first real interest in my kind, and it engrossed me wholly. I had seen her,—I should see her,—and my mind lay steeped in the visions that flowed from this source. My task-work I went through with, as I have done on similar occasions all my life, aided by pride that could not bear to fail, or be questioned. Could I cease from doing the work of the day, and hear the reason sneeringly given,—' Her head is so com-

pletely taken up with ———— that she can do nothing?'
Impossible . . . I can tell little else of this time,—
indeed, I remember little, except the state of feeling
in which I lived."

She was unable to cope with her excessive grief
when the stranger went away. "Those who are really
children could not know such love, or feel such sorrow," she comments. She fell into a complete hysterical innervation,—"I knew not how to exert myself,
but lay bound hand and foot,"—and soon took refuge
in outright sickness. The robust and energetic girl
was genuinely ill.

For the first time, her father began to suspect that
there was something wrong. He suddenly discovered
that she needed to be with girls of her own age. But
already the Cambridge girls were hostile towards the
eccentric Margaret, and so she was sent away to boarding school. The school selected was that of the Misses
Prescott, in Groton, Massachusetts. Here Margaret
spent her fourteenth and fifteenth years, and her experiences there are told in the story of a fictitious
"Marianna," who "irritated the girls, as all eccentric-
ity does the world in general, more than vice or
malignity." Groton was, of course, no kinder than
Cambridge,—the only difference being that the girl
was forced into a hand-to-hand struggle with public
opinion. She soon learned which was the stronger.

Her father had delivered her up to a most unequal combat.

The climax came as the result of a series of theatricals in which Margaret's abilities and talents naturally brought her to the fore. The principal parts fell to her as a matter of course and for a time she reigned triumphant. But the plays came to an end and the gray commonplace régime again prevailed. But Margaret, after the plays were over, kept on painting her cheeks. The girls jeered at her, and Margaret defended herself at first, saying she thought it made her look pretty. Then she became stubborn and silent—but kept up the habit. In her story, Margaret gives no reason for Marianna's behavior, and probably she knew none; but the famous peach-bloom on her mother's cheeks, so celebrated in family annals, was doubtless at the bottom of the girl's absurdity. She could not stop for the simple reason that she did not know why she did it.

Margaret's schoolmates did not understand her. She infuriated them, as only the eccentric can infuriate the blessed normal people. They decided to punish her and enlisted the teachers in their conspiracy. One day she came down to dinner to find all the girls deeply rouged with round, glaring spots on their cheeks. As her eyes traveled around the table, she saw that every one had joined the trick against her. Even the teachers smiled and the servants tittered. The world despised her and triumphed in her disgrace! She gave no sign during the meal, but afterwards she went to her room and fell upon the floor in convulsions. Instantly, everybody was kind and attentive, and the episode passed over.

Margaret left off painting her cheeks, but the memory of how not one person had taken her part rankled within her. Now that she was beaten and outwardly subdued, her schoolmates became more friendly and gave her their confidences. In a spirit of revenge the girl saw her chance to create dissension among them and used it. She began her deliberate mischief-making with prudence but grew so bold with her success that she ran into a second fiasco. She was called upon by the principal to answer charges to be preferred against her. Marianna stood up and leaned against the chimney-piece, while eight of the older girls came forward and charged her with falsehood and calumny. The outcome was more convulsions and another illness. Her feeling of revenge had given place to a feeling of remorse, and the poor distracted girl became more hysterical than ever in the herd-atmosphere of the Misses Prescott's school.

Margaret was fifteen when she returned from boarding school and sixteen when her father gave the famous party for John Quincy Adams. She wore a pink silk dress on that occasion and presented the appearance of a buxom young woman of eighteen. From this time forth, she was " out." She was a marriageable young woman and she now went into society. Higginson says she " danced through college " with the class of 1829. But not all of them would dance with her; they found her too dashing, too aggressive, and too talkative. Aside from one " disappointment," no love affairs developed. It began to appear that she was destined for spinsterhood. The natural conclusion in the observer's mind, and doubtless in Margaret's own, was that the young men of her own generation had passed her by. When maids do not marry, of course, it is because they are " plain." Margaret " made up her mind to be bright and ugly." The theory of sex-attraction was very simple in those days—beauty in women and bravery in men made it all so simple.

Margaret's passions found some outlet in that particular form of self-love which is known as ambition. She was madly ambitious. " I feel the power of industry growing every day, and, besides the all-powerful motive of ambition, and a new stimulus lately given through a friend, I have learned to believe that nothing, no! not perfection, is unattainable. I am determined on distinction, which formerly I thought to win at an easy rate; but now I see that long years of labor must be given to secure even the ' succès de societé '—which, however, shall never content me. I see multitudes of examples of persons of genius, utterly deficient in grace and the power of pleasurable excitement. I wish to combine both. I know the obstacles in my way. I am wanting in that intuitive tact and polish, which nature has bestowed upon some, but which I must acquire. And, on the other hand, my powers of intellect, though sufficient, I suppose, are not well disciplined. Yet all such hindrances may be overcome by an ardent spirit. If I fail, my conso-lation shall be found in active employment." The writer of these lines was just fifteen. It is already easy to foresee that she would not deserve to be called "a true woman " on her tombstone.

In order to produce that glorious Margaret of to-morrow to whom the Margaret of today was as the dull caterpillar is to the gorgeous butterfly, the girl toiled indefatigably. She wrote to her teacher: " I rise a little before five, walk an hour, and then practice on the piano, till seven, when we have breakfast. Next I read French—Sismondi's *Literature of the South of Europe,*—till eight, then two or three lectures in Brown's *Philosophy.* About half-past nine I go to Mr. Perkin's school and study Greek till twelve, when, the school being dismissed, I recite, go home, and prac-tice again till dinner, at two. Sometimes, if the conversation is very agreeable, I lounge for half an hour over the dessert, though rarely so lavish of time. Then, when I can, I read two hours in Italian, but I am often interrupted. At six, I walk, or take a drive. Before going to bed, I play or sing for half an hour or so, to make all sleepy, and, about eleven, retire to write a little while in my journal, exercises on what I have read, or a series of characteristics which I am filling up according to advice. Thus, you see, I am learning Greek, and making acquaintance with metaphysics, and French and Italian literature."

Margaret was going to be sixteen next week, and she had a great decision to make. " Now tell me," she wrote to her teacher, " had you rather be the brilliant de Stael or the useful Edgeworth?" It was a mere rhetorical question, for the brilliant de Stael was an easy winner,—the daughter of Necker who had published at the age of fifteen a remarkable defense of her father's political conduct and whose ruling passion through life had been her filial devotion. De Stael was plain; she was a brilliant conversationalist, a distinguished author, and an able politician. Yes, a de Stael would do as an incentive, but one must work prodigiously. Margaret attacked her studies, as she said, with a " gladiatorial disposition."

She liked a companion in her studies, but there were few who could stand her pace. In Lydia Maria

Francis, a fellow-disciple of the brilliant de Stael, she found a friend and the two seventeen-year-old girls read together and conversed loftily on metaphysics and politics. At nineteen, she attached to herself James Freeman Clarke as a friend to whom she could speak of her studies. They rode together on horseback from Cambridge to Newton and discussed all day long socialism, friendship, and the power of circumstances. When Carlyle made German literature the fashion, they fell to and learned German together, and within three months, according to the young man's account, Margaret was reading with ease all the masterpieces which Carlyle had reviewed and many others besides. Probably Carlyle himself, in his remote Craigenputtock, had learned the language no faster than did this new disciple in her narrow New England corner. With Frederick Henry Hedge, another platonic friend, she embarked upon ambitious schemes of translations from the German, which led to some excellent literary work from both. To William Henry Channing, Margaret confided "her secret hope of what Woman might be and do, as an author, in our Republic." She sketched a portrait which Channing recognized as her own and, he adds, "we were strangers no more." They were united in the free-masonry of the ambitious.

Though Margaret could read Latin and German and compare ambitions with these young men, she could not make love to them. But it was a necessity of her nature to make love to somebody. She solved the dilemma in the usual way. " She was one of those maidens," says Higginson, " who form passionate attachments to older women." He describes how she paid court to his mother and other staid matrons of Cambridge. One of her idols, a certain Mrs. Farrar, who was the author of a *Manual for Young Ladies,* took her in hand and polished up her manners, which, according to Margaret's own account, were much in need of an expert's touch. She wooed young women also. There was the beautiful Anna Barker whom she adored but who filled her with such despairing envy that Margaret struggled with curl-papers night after night when French and metaphysics had had their due. What seemed so hard for Margaret seemed so easy for Anna. The young men paid her court and in the proper season, she married one of them. But probably Anna had not been elected in her cradle to be the companion of her father.

Margaret was accused of sentimentalism and romantic exaggeration in her friendships. She belonged to an age which reveled in Rousseau, Bettina Brentano, and de Stael, and the grafting of foreign romanticism on the native Puritan stock sometimes produced outlandish results. But for all that, Margaret was a sincere student of the romantic impulse and her observations were accurate so far as they went. She was one of those who stood as sign-posts along the road which was to lead in time to a scientific view of the nature of love. " It is so true that a woman may be in love with a woman, and a man with a man. It is pleasant to be sure of it, because it is undoubtedly the same love that we shall feel when we are angels, when we ascend to the only fit place for the Mignons, where ' sie fragen nicht nach Mann und Weib '. It is regulated by the same law as that of love between persons of different sexes, only it is purely intellectual and spiritual, unprofaned by any mixture of lower instincts, undisturbed by any need of consulting temporal interests; its law is the desire of the spirit to realize a whole, which makes it seek in another being that which it finds not in itself. Thus the beautiful seek the strong, the mute seek the eloquent; the butterfly settles on the dark flower. Why did Socrates love Alcibiades? Why did Kaiser so love Schneider? How natural is the love of Wallenstein for Max, that of Madame de Stael for de Recamier, mine for ——! I loved —— for a time with as much passion as I was then strong enough to feel. Her face was always gleaming before me; her voice was echoing in my ear. All poetic thoughts clustered round the dear image. . . . She loved me, for I well remember her suffering when she first could feel my faults, and knew one part of the exquisite veil rent away—how she wished to stay apart and weep the whole day." It is worth noticing that Margaret here hit upon what is said by the modern Freudian to be one of the chief ear-marks of this form of love, and that is a greater mutual sensitiveness to faults than exists in the more mature form of love between persons of opposite sexes.

Through these experiences of hers, Margaret was led to make a translation of the Bettina-Günderode letters soon after their publication in Leipzig in 1840. The Canoness Günderode is perhaps less famous than her masculine counterpart, the melancholy Werther, but she suffered from the same kind of Weltschmerz and threw herself into the river Rhine. The correspondence between her and Bettina Brentano is full of ecstatic poetry of which Margaret was able, largely through her sympathy, to make an excellent English rendering. She met Günderode at a turning-point in her life and for a year or so followed her as a model. She turned her back upon the world and sought for consolation in a life of mysticism.

Despite her strong instinct for action and her extraordinary energy, she seemed to languish at home without an aim in life. The family fortunes were declining and yet she made no effort to find an occupation for herself. In those years there were few occupations open to women, and yet it seems as if Margaret with her unusual energies might have found something to do even then. She longed to travel, then why not strike out for Virginia to be a governess on a plantation? But she stuck at home like any spiritless spinster of her time. She longed for love and marriage, and yet she took no steps to satisfy her longing. Of course she was a perfect lady, and a perfect lady did not go husband-hunting. Yet she was far from shrinking in her other relationships. When she had marked a person for her friend, says Emerson, the one so marked could not escape. " Persons were her game, specially if marked by fortune, or character, or success—to such was she sent. . . . Indeed they fell in her way, when the access might have seemed difficult, by wonderful casualties." If she was such a successful adventuress as all this, why did she not acquire a husband by the same method? It was just there, apparently, that her instinct for possession failed her completely.

She sat in a prison of her own making. " All hopes of traveling I have dismissed," she wrote in her Journal. " All youthful hopes, of every kind, I have pushed from my thoughts. I will not, if I can help it, lose an hour in castle-building and repining—too much of that already. I have now a pursuit of immediate importance: to the German language and literature I will give my undivided attention. I have made rapid progress for one quite unassisted. I have always hitherto been too constantly distracted by childish feelings to acquire anything properly, but have snatched a little here and there to feed my restless fancy therewith. Please God now to keep my mind composed, that I may store it with all that may be conducive to the best good of others. Oh, keep me steady in an honorable ambition; favored by this calm, this obscurity of life, I might learn everything, did not feeling lavish away my strength."

Soon after this, and quite suddenly, came her father's decision to retire upon a farm. Margaret was appalled by the prospect, yet it never occurred to her to find a way of remaining in Boston.

CHAPTER IV

MIRANDA

THE Fuller farm was only forty miles from Boston, but there was no railway in those days and country life represented a real exile to Margaret. Miranda greeted her desert isle with a flood of bitter tears. Nevertheless she unpacked her trunks, and settled in for life: there was now no other prospect visible.

She was only doing what custom required of unmarried daughters in those days. One by one the boys would grow up and leave, but she would always stay on in the Groton farmhouse. In Boston she had already a " circle " and several Platonic friendships. She had been reading German with Henry Hedge, but now she read the letters of Thomas Jefferson with her father. " I rejoice, if only because my father and I can have so much in common on this topic," she wrote to Hedge; " all my other pursuits have led me away from him; here he has much information and ripe judgment." Together they delved into Latin again, and Margaret wrote a long " defense of Brutus " which was published in a Boston newspaper. It was replied to by some learned " big-wig " of Salem, who would have been greatly humiliated no doubt could he have known that his opponent in this duel of Latin quotations was a young woman of twenty-four. Margaret's father was immensely proud of her.

He gave into her hands the education of the younger children. There were younger brothers to be prepared for college, and to this end Margaret kept school five days in the week and her school day was from five to eight hours long. Incidentally she renewed her reading of Virgil and reflected a good deal on his masculine women and his anti-religious ideas of heaven and virtue. She watched her pupils as they tried to reconcile Virgil with the Sunday morning sermon and recalled her own struggles. " I really find it difficult," she wrote to a friend, " to keep their *morale* steady, and am inclined to think many of my skeptical sufferings are traceable to this source." To another friend she wrote, " I will tell you how I pass my time without society or exercise. Even till two o'clock, sometimes later, I pour ideas into the heads of the little Fullers; much runs out, but the few drops which remain mightily gladden the sight of my father." Her labors were lightened also by the promise of a European tour. Her father had promised her this as a reward for her school-keeping.

At the same time, Margaret was in no way exempt from the household cares of the grown-up daughter.

She sewed and swept and nursed the sick. Her mother fell ill; her invalid grandmother came to spend the winter; one of the children had a serious accident and a long convalescence; and the baby of the family fell sick and died. Once when William Channing took Margaret to task for her arrogance she replied, " Remember that only through aspirations, which sometimes make me what is called unreasonable, have I been enabled to vanquish unpropitious circumstances and save my soul alive."

The family atmosphere at Groton was darkened by new currents of hostile feeling. Margaret's brothers were nearing maturity and the old strife between father and son broke out in the household. Margaret says that " collisions with his elder sons, which would not have ended there," embittered the last days of her father. Having spoiled his daughter, he now fought with his sons. Eugene, the eldest, went to Virginia as a tutor on a plantation and ultimately made his way to New Orleans and a journalist's career. The second son followed, and only the little boys remained. The patriarch was left practically alone with his women-folk.

But there was now a conflict between himself and his daughter. She would not be reconciled to the farm. She would not even look at it; rather would she go without exercise than survey the crops and fields and her father's improvements on the place. He wished to build her a rustic seat, where she might go and read alone, but she always put him off when it came to selecting the spot. In this way, the petty but poignant battle went on between them.

Margaret sustained the emotional conflict for two years and then fell desperately ill. Her life was despaired of by the family and she herself believed that she was near death. Her poor mother tended her for nine days and nights without intermission At last her father came into the sick-room and said, " My dear, I have been thinking of you in the night, and I cannot remember you have any *faults*. You have defects, of course, as all mortals have, but I do not know that you have a single fault." As her father had always acted on the belief that praise was hurtful to children, this declaration was a momentous event. It shattered the habit of a lifetime, and Margaret could feel that victory was hers. She began to recover.

Soon after this, her father fell ill and died very suddenly of Asiatic cholera. His daughter, not his wife, closed his eyes in death.

Margaret was filled with remorse. " My father's image follows me constantly. Whenever I am in my room, he seems to open the door, and to look on me with a complacent smile." But she was now the head of the family in earnest and prepared to imitate the self-sacrificing parent whose mantle she had inherited. "I have often had reason to regret being of the softer sex," she said, "and never more than now. If I were an oldest son, I could be guardian to my brothers and sister, administer the estate, and really become the head of the family." But her father's business affairs had to be taken care of by Uncle Abraham, and so the power was divided. "Prospero gave Miranda a scepter, not his wand," was the way Margaret described the situation.

The European trip was off. There was not enough money, and Margaret's small portion would not be available for some time to come. In the meantime, Harriet Martineau was about to return to England with Mrs. Farrar, the author of the *Manual for Young Ladies,* and Margaret had been invited to return with the party. But Uncle Abraham soon showed her that this was impossible. Everybody was sorry for poor Margaret. Harriet Martineau was especially sorry, but Emerson rebuked her: "Does Margaret Fuller, supposing her to be what you say, believe her progress to be dependent on whether she is here or there?" Margaret thought it did; nevertheless she decided, after much agonizing, not to forsake her family. Her self-sacrifice was greatly admired by her friends and much celebrated by her biographers. But Margaret, who had a truthful nature, wrote to her brother some years afterwards, "Probably, if I had been aware at the time of what I was doing, I might not have sacrificed myself so."

But she no longer contemplated a future on the farm. One evening, while calling on some poor neighbors in Groton, she had a vision that stirred her to action. "The moon tempted me out, and I set forth for a house at no great distance . . . I will try to give you an impression of what you, I fancy, have never come in contact with. The little room—they have but one—contains a bed, a table, and some old chairs. A single stick of wood burns in the fireplace. It is not needed now, but those who sit near it have long ceased to know what spring is. They are all frost. Everything is old and faded, but at the same time as clean and carefully mended as possible. For all they know of pleasure is to get strength to sweep those few boards, and mend those old spreads and curtains. That sort of self-respect they have, and it is all of pride their many years of poor-tithe has left them.

"And there they sit,—mother and daughter. In the mother, ninety years have quenched every thought and every feeling, except an imbecile interest about her daughter, and the sort of self-respect I just spoke of. Husband, sons, strength, health, house and lands, all are gone. And yet those losses have not had power to bow that palsied head to the grave. Morning by morning, she rises without a hope, night by night she lies down vacant or apathetic. . . . We look on this dry leaf, and think how green it was, and how the birds sung to it in its summer day.

" But can we think of spring, or summer, or anything joyous or really life-like, when we look at the daughter?—that bloodless effigy of humanity, whose care is to eke out this miserable existence by means of the occasional doles of those who know how faithful and good a child she has been to that decrepit creature. . . . The saddest part is, that she does *not wish* for death. She clings to this sordid existence. Her soul is now so habitually enwrapt in the meanest cares, that if she were to be lifted two or three steps upward, she would not know what to do with her life; how, then, shall she soar to the celestial heights? Yet she ought; for she has ever been good, and her crushing duties have been performed with a self-sacrificing constancy, which I, for one, could never hope to equal."

A short time after writing this sketch, Margaret was looking for a job. She found one as a teacher of languages in Mr. Alcott's school. She gave private lessons as well and translated De Wette and Herder evenings for Dr. Channing. Her cherished plan was to write a life of Goethe; but the Alcott school soon failed and Margaret left Boston to teach in Providence,

Rhode Island. The ambitious idea of writing a life of Goethe was exchanged for the more modest task of translating *Eckermann's Conversations*. Goethe at that time enjoyed a very unsavory reputation in New England. Longfellow expressed the general feeling in a lecture at Harvard, " What I most object to in the old gentleman is his sensuality." And even Emerson could not forbear joining in the popular disgust. " The Puritan in me accepts no apology for bad morals in such as he," he said. Considering all this adverse feeling, Margaret's solitary and unsupported enthusiasm for the disreputable old gentleman must have seemed at least unwomanly. She wrote a defense of Goethe, which was published as an introduction to her *Eckermann's Conversations* and which still ranks as one of the best pieces of Goethe criticism extant.

In Providence, Margaret led an active life. She called herself the " Lady Superior " of her school, still evidently under the spell of the Canoness Günderode, but she did not fully espouse the part. She went to political meetings and envied the political orators. A French man-of-war, anchored in the bay, stirred her imagination. " I thought I much should like to command such a vessel, despite all the hardships and privations of such a situation." She horrified the director of her school by attending a Whig Caucus and wrote to a friend, " It is rather the best thing I have done."

The school-mistress began to feel herself a citizen of the world.

At last the farm was sold, and Margaret returned home for a rest until the new tenants should take possession in the spring. She returned in the midst of the wintry snows and devoted her " rest " period to almost constant invalidism. After her active life in Providence, she became a sickly, aging spinster,— one of the tragic and benumbed sisterhood, of whom Elizabeth Barrett wrote—

> " How dreary 'tis for women to sit still
> On winter nights, by solitary fires,
> And hear the nations praising them far off."

When she at last escaped from the clutches of the farm and moved her family to Jamaica Plain, near Boston, she wrote to Emerson triumphantly, " This day I write from my own hired house and am full of the dignity of citizenship. Really, it is almost happiness."

Presently Margaret woke up to discover that she was thirty and life still unaccountably passed her by. " Tonight I lay on the sofa," she wrote, " and saw how the flame shot up from beneath, through the mass of coal that had been piled above. It shot up in wild, beautiful jets, and then unexpectedly sank again, and all was black, unsightly, and forlorn. And thus, I thought, is it with my life at present. Yet if the fire beneath persists and conquers, that dead mass will become all radiant, life-giving, fit for the altar on the domestic hearth. Yes, and it shall be so." At times she tried to persuade herself that she was willing to postpone the whole thing until another incarnation. " Please, good genius of my life, to make me very patient, resolute, gentle, while no less ardent; and after having tried me well, please present, at the end of some thousand years or so, a sphere of congenial and consecutive labors; of heart-felt, heart-filling wishes carried out into life on the instant." But then at other times she felt that any delay at all was danger-ous. " Once I was almost all intellect," she wrote, " now I am almost all feeling. Nature vindicates her rights, and I feel all Italy glowing beneath the Saxon crust. This cannot last long; I shall burn to ashes if all this smolders here much longer. I must die if I do not burst forth in genius or heroism."

In her desperation she confided her longing to the dead Beethoven. Returning from the symphony, she sat down at her desk and wrote: " My only friend;—How shall I thank thee for one more breaking the chains of my sorrowful slumber? My heart beats. I live again, for I feel that I am worthy audience for thee, and that my being would be reason enough for thine. Master, my eyes are always clear. I see that

the universe is rich, if I am poor. I see the insignifi-
cance of my sorrows. In my will, I am not a captive;
in my intellect, not a slave. Is it then my fault that the
palsy of my affections benumbs my whole life?

" I know that the curse is but for the time. I know
what the eternal justice promises. But on this one
sphere, it is sad. Thou didst say, thou hadst no friend
but thy art. But that one is enough. I have no art,
in which to vent the swell of a soul as deep as thine,
Beethoven, and of a kindred frame. Thou wilt not
think me presumptuous in this saying, as another
might. I have always known that thou wouldst wel-
come and know me, as would no other who ever lived
upon this earth since its first creation. Thou wouldst
forgive me, master, that I have not been true to my
eventual destiny, and therefore have suffered on every
side ' the pangs of despised love.' Thou didst the
same, but thou didst borrow from these errors the
inspiration of thy genius. Why is it not thus with me?
Is it because, as a woman, I am bound by a physical
law, which prevents the soul from manifesting itself?
Sometimes the moon seems mockingly to say so—to
say that I, too, shall not shine, unless I find a sun.
O, cold and barren moon, tell a different tale!

" But thou, oh blessed master! dost answer all my
questions, and make it my privilege to be. Like a
humble wife to the sage, or poet, it is my triumph

that I can understand and cherish thee: like a mistress, I arm thee for the fight; like a young daughter, I tenderly bind thy wounds. Thou art to me beyond compare, for thou art all I want. No heavenly sweetness of saint or martyr, no many leaved Raphael, no golden Plato, is anything to me compared with thee. The infinite Shakespeare, the stern Angelo, Dante—bittersweet like thee—are no longer seen in thy presence. And besides these names, there are none that could vibrate in thy crystal sphere. Thou hast all of them, and that ample surge of life besides, that great winged being which they only dreamed of. There is none greater than Shakespeare; he, too, is a god; but his creations are successive; thy *fiat* comprehends them all. . . .

"Master, I have this summer envied the oriole which had even a swinging nest in the high bough. I have envied the least flower that came to seed, though that seed were strown to the wind. But I envy none when I am with thee.". . .

Steeped in the seductive mysticism of Novalis, Margaret tried to find consolation for her surcharged longings in a life of visions. But she was by no means a success as a mystic, her tendency being, as she put it, "rather to a great natural than a deep religious life." Nevertheless, she was not to leave that experience untried. In the summer of 1840 she isolated herself completely, hoping to learn the lesson of renunciation through communion with ideal spirits and celestial loves. She declared that she achieved a state of ecstasy and a haven of spiritual peace. But soon after she was writing, " Renunciation appears to be complete, and I am quite content; yet, probably, 'tis no such thing, and that work is to be done over and over again." In this surmise, she was altogether correct.

At this time of her life, Margaret cultivated a demon. Goethe also had a demon and so did Socrates but Emerson did not. He was profoundly irritated by demons, but Margaret insisted on telling him the news of hers. " With me for weeks and months the demon works his will," she declared. To keep her demon company, she built up " a little mythology of her own," in which anniversaries and symbols were seriously considered. She adopted the carbuncle for her favorite stone and the sistrum for her emblem. Her definition of the demoniacal was taken from Goethe, but she explained it in her own way thus: " In genius and in character, it works . . . instinctively; it refuses to be analyzed by the understanding, and is most of all inaccessible to the person who possesses it. We can only say, I have it, he has it. . . . It has given rise to the fables of wizard, enchantress, and the like; these beings are scarcely good, yet not necessarily bad. Power tempts them." Thus she tried to analyze the power of the unconscious, that unknown and inexplicable force,—repressed yet irrepressible, forgotten but indestructible,—by which she felt herself enthralled but which was at the same time the source of all her energy. Modern psychology has fully justified her analysis of the source of her creative energy and accounted for the resistance on the part of Emerson, himself incapable of abandon, to the recognition of a power which defied a rationalistic explanation.

Besides her demon, she cultivated a midnight personality whom she called "Leila." To Leila she addressed herself in a sketch which appeared in an early issue of *The Dial*. "I did not love thee, Leila, but the desire for love was soothed in thy presence." She describes her dealings with the dream-world through Leila. "At night I look into the lake for Leila. If I gaze steadily and in the singleness of prayer, she rises and walks on its depths. Then know I each night a part of her life; I know where she passes the midnight hours. In the day she lives among men; she observes their deeds, and gives them what they want of her, justice or love. . . . In the night she wanders forth from her human investment, and travels amid these tribes, freer movers in the game of spirit and matter, to whom this man is a supplement. I know not

then whether she is what men call dreaming, but her
life is true, full, and more single than by day. . . .

" They say that such purity is the seal of death.
It is so; the condition of this ecstasy is, that it seems
to die every moment, and even Leila has not force to
die often; the electricity accumulates many days before
the wild one comes, which leads to these sylph nights
of tearful sweetness. After one of these, I find her
always to have retreated into the secret veins of earth.
Then glows through her whole being the fire that so
baffles men, as she walks on the surface of the earth;
the blood-red, heart's-blood-red of the universal heart,
with no care except to circulate as the vital fluid; and it
would seem waste then for her to rise to the surface."

Frustrated in her affections, brooding over her
famine in the midst of plenty, Margaret found that
she could at least indulge herself in fantasies and
reveries. These treasured unrealities were the aftermath of her father's death. The whole thing was a
process of self-cheating. She thought that she would
achieve happiness by a renunciation which was after
all no renunciation. It was, on the contrary, an indulgence in a visionary clinging to a companionship
which belonged to the past. " How often has the
spirit chosen the time, when no ray came from without,
to descend upon the orphan life," she wrote in her
Journal. " The great spirit wished to leave me no

refuge but itself." Her phenomenal energies were running to waste in pathological quicksands, and she tampered with her mental health as at other times she had tampered with her physical health. She abandoned herself to charms and spells, to symbolism and mysticism, employing such things as a means of reviving within herself certain childish states of feeling, which were all she knew of happiness. With a flash of insight, she one day declared in her Journal that " in feeling, she was still a child."

From this desert of the early thirties, Margaret was in time to emerge pretty completely. But it was just during this period of her life that her relations with Emerson were intimate, and he always saw her in this character. But whether she languished among her visions or actually betook herself to a sick bed, she displayed an amount of energy which astounded him. " She had a rude strength, which, if it could have been supported by an equal health, would have given her the efficiency of the strongest man," he said. He declared that he could not vie with her in the volume of work that she turned out in spite of her frequent disability. Yet neither he nor any of the others seemed to waste much time over the anomalous combination of frail health and inexhaustible energy. It did not strike them as anything suspicious or inexplicable. There were many such heroines of the sick bed in the early Victorian and late Puritan era, so that Margaret's case was not entirely unique.

Apparently she realized that it would cost her a long and weary process to adapt herself to normal life. Her muscular personality could not imitate the ethereal Günderode. Discordant action was always preferable to her to stoical inaction. Therefore she compared herself to a sistrum, a triangular musical instrument which is induced to produce musical sounds by being ceaselessly agitated, and she wrote these verses to her emblem :—

> " Triune, shaping, restless power,
> Life-flow from life's natal hour,
> No music chords are in thy sound;
> By some thou'rt but a rattle found;
> Yet, without thy ceaseless motion,
> To ice would turn their dead devotion.

> " Life-flow of my natal hour,
> I will not weary of thy power,
> Till in the changes of thy sound,
> A chord's three parts distinct are found.
> I will faithful move with thee,
> God-ordered, self-fed energy,
> Nature in eternity."

CHAPTER V

A WOMAN'S WOMAN

MARGARET emerged into public life as a woman's woman. In her individual relationships, she exhibited, of course, the same characteristic. She inspired other women with enthusiastic discipleship, which was sometimes hard for men to understand, especially if they happened to be the husbands of her disciples. Horace Greeley spoke with great asperity of the fascination which she seemed to exert over eminent and cultivated women, who came to his out-of-the-way dwelling to visit her, and who seemed generally " to regard her with a strangely Oriental adoration." In other words, Mr. Greeley could not fathom the attraction she had for his wife.

Margaret Fuller's feminism represents the socialization of a part of that " instinctive life ", which, contrary to her Puritan upbringing, she had learned to recognize and value. The feminism of women, like the corresponding form of sex-solidarity among men, is based on a social impulse which is in turn, rooted in an erotic impulse towards others of one's own sex. The destruction of this impulse is neither possible nor desirable. Women who are unfriendly and unsympathetic toward the mass problems of their own sex are defective on this side of their emotional development. Somewhere along the road of their evolving characters, they have lost the capacity for a social emotion of a very high value.

Margaret's life was a better argument for woman's rights than anything she ever wrote. What she said of Mary Wollstonecraft and George Sand applied with equal truth to herself. " Mary Wollstonecraft, like . . . George Sand in our day, was a woman whose existence proved the need of some new interpretation of woman's rights more than anything she wrote. Such beings as these, rich in genius, of most tender sympathies, capable of high virtue and a chastened harmony, ought not to find themselves, by birth, in a place so narrow, that in breaking bonds, they become outlaws."

In this sense, Margaret too was an outlaw. She was hedged about by a prejudice and misrepresentation which almost assumed the character of a social boycott. She shared the fate of every famous woman from Sappho onward, who has set an example of emancipation for their sex. People who did not know Margaret in Boston, avoided an introduction, and, but for her own athletic efforts to prevent it, she would have been well isolated.

Among her own sex, Margaret never lacked for champions. Though Mr. Greeley was mystified by her influence over women, Mr. Higginson had a simple explanation for it. " Margaret Fuller loved music, painting, and women," said he, " and understood the last."

She studied the conditions of women's lives and recorded her observations with the accuracy and objectivity which belongs to modern social research. " The observations of women upon the position of women are always more valuable than those of men," she said. Wherever she traveled, Margaret never failed to remark the facts about the women—their appearance, their behavior, their social position. Now it would be the Indian squaws whom she saw near Chicago. " With the women I held much communication by signs," she wrote. " They are almost invariably coarse and ugly, with the exception of their eyes, with a peculiarly awkward gait, and forms bent by burdens. This gait, so different from the steady and noble step of the men, marks the inferior position they occupy." Compare this with her impression of Italian women written seven years later. " The women of Arles," she said, " answered to their reputation for beauty; tall, erect, and noble, with high and dignified features, and a full earnest gaze of the eye. . . . Even the very old women still have a degree of beauty because when the colors are all faded, and the skin wrinkled, the face retains this dignity of outline. The men do not share in these characteristics. Some priestess, well-beloved of the powers of old religion, must have called down a special blessing on her sisters in this town."

Everywhere she commented on the character of women's work. The life of the Illinois farmer's wife, the washer-women of New York, the weavers of Lancashire and Lyons—all women who earned their bread were closely observed by her. During her stay in New York she helped to organize the first protective association for prostitutes and she carried on for years a study of the social and economic causes of prostitution. Writing from Paris, she said, " I have collected many facts with regard to this suffering class of women, both in England and in France. . . . I have seen the feelings of men with regard to their condition and the general heartlessness in women of more favored and protected lives, which I can only ascribe to utter ignorance of the facts. If a proclamation of some of these can remove it, I hope to make such a one in the hour of riper judgment, and after a more extensive survey." And, still later, writing about Italy, she said that the subjection of women there had sharpened her perceptions to the ills of women's condition and the remedies that must be applied, adding, " Had I but genius, had I but energy, to tell what I know as it ought to be told." As Higginson said, she loved women and knew them, and to the end of her life she served with earnestness and sincerity the world-wide community of her sex.

The famous " Conversations " which she held in Boston from 1839 to 1844, were really an experiment in feminism. Casting about for an occupation and a career, the idea of a " paid Corinne " naturally presented itself. She was one of the best impromptu talkers of her time, and it was an era of great talkers. Coleridge and Carlyle were Titans with the tongue and, in America, Alcott, Channing, and Emerson were the leaders of a talkers' guild which centered around Concord. It was just the time for Margaret to try her luck as an improvisatrice, for her demon had a brilliant turn for all this kind of thing. As far back as her boarding-school days, when the fifteen-year-old girl would spin like a Dervish and then suddenly halt and improvise, her demon had been preparing her for this career. She said candidly about herself : " Conversation is my natural element. I need to be called out, and never think alone, without imagining some companion. Whether this be nature or the force of circumstances, I know not; it is my habit, and bespeaks a second-rate mind." For all her ambition and her alleged self-esteem she was perfectly willing to face her own limitations.

Her scheme of Conversations addressed itself to women and to women only. The purpose was, as her prospectus said, "to supply a point of union to well-educated and thinking women, in a city, which, with great pretensions to mental refinement, boasts, at present, nothing of the kind." Thus she set out to imitate Aspasia, corrupting the women of Athens by means of intellectual orgies. The prospectus continues to outline Margaret's aim, which is to counteract the bad education of her sex. Her ambition is "to systematize thought and give a precision and clearness in which our sex are so deficient, chiefly, I think, because they have so few inducements to test and classify what they receive. To ascertain what pursuits are best suited to us, in our time and state of society, and how we may make best use of our means for building up the life of thought upon the life of action." In her introductory meeting, she expanded her text more fully. "Women are now taught, at school, all that men are. . . . But with this difference; men are called on, from a very early period to reproduce all that they learn. Their college exercises, their political duties, their professional studies, the first actions of life in any direction, call on them to put to use what they have learned. But women learn without any attempt to reproduce. Their only reproduction is for purposes of display." Yet Margaret's Conversations are usually spoken of as a purely literary affair instead of the feminist adventure which they really were.

The original class of twenty-five "ladies" came together in Elizabeth Peabody's rooms in West Street. The first series of talks was on " Grecian Mythology; " the second, on " The Fine Arts; " the third, on " Woman." There was one isolated conversation which dealt with " Persons who never awake to life in this world." There must have been a number of Boston ladies present who could have contributed something on this theme. Margaret's talks were mainly drawn from Goethe's philosophy of life, from whom she had derived a heterodox attitude on the subject of " moral evil " which was sometimes very disturbing to the ladies of her class. But the talks on " Woman: Her Position in the Family, in the School, in the Church and in Society " embodied a composite critique which must have been built up very largely out of the thoughts and personal experiences of those present. The outcome of the class was Margaret's book on *Woman in the Nineteenth Century,* which in its turn prepared the way for the Seneca Falls Convention of 1848 and the woman's rights conventions of the '50's.

The new class, which included the feminine intelligentsia of Boston, became naturally the butt of wits and the prey of scoffers. Their pretensions were derided and the leader was put down as a "pedant." Margaret's crowning offense, in the eyes of the philistines, was that she arrayed herself to look her best on these occasions and her disciples naïvely imitated her "dressiness." Harriet Martineau, in a fit of pique against her former friend, once described Margaret's group as "gorgeous pedants." All this criticism grew out of the fact that her young admirers came away delighted with "her beautiful looks" and her "sumptuous dress." Emerson tried to refute these accusations, which he took very seriously, by protesting that he personally knew that Margaret did not over-spend herself on dress and that she could not possibly have looked beautiful. He admitted that the "impression of her genius" might have "obscured her homeliness of feature." But he did not admit that the adoration of her young friends might have imparted a glamour to its object such as affection is accustomed to impart. The Puritan in him might allow for the play of genius, but not for the play of a perfectly natural feeling which made these women like to dress to please each other.

A great impetus to the woman movement in this country was given by the anti-slavery convention in

London. The exclusion of the women from the floor stirred Elizabeth Cady Stanton and Lucretia Mott profoundly and gave the impulse to the protest which was voiced by the Seneca Falls Convention eight years later. In Mrs. Stanton's account of this historic event, she says of Lucretia Mott, " I shall never forget the look of recognition she gave me when she saw by my remarks that I fully comprehended the problem of woman's rights and wrongs. How beautiful she looked to me that day! " This would seem to indicate that the same kind of emotional sympathy was at work in this contemporary group which characterized the atmosphere of the conversation class. Of course this sentiment was frowned upon by people who found it perfectly normal and moral, on the other hand, that women should be antagonistic and competitive in their relations with other women. In the same way they have stigmatized all affection among men until a modern psychologist like Ferenczi declares that, " to an astounding extent, present-day men have lost the capacity for mutual affection and amiability." This attitude assumes that ill-will among men and ill-will among women are the only basis for good-will between the sexes, whereas it should be evident that social good-will cannot possibly obtain on a basis of resistance and antagonism within a whole sex. But when Margaret Fuller taught, in the words of

Antigone, that "the aim of women is not to hate but to love each other," there were many who hastened to construe this as "the aim of women is not to love but to hate men." Nothing was more foreign to Margaret's real feeling. She was, in fact, a very poor hater of anybody; she had few personal quarrels and few resentments.

After the Conversations had been going for a year or so and had proved a great success, it was proposed that gentlemen should be admitted. Margaret had the very practical idea that the advantages of a Harvard training would enable them to contribute an element of strength to the discussions of Mythology which the feeble learning of the ladies necessarily could not supply. So an arrangement for evening classes was made and the gentlemen were invited to participate. But somehow the scheme did not prosper, and the masculine contingent hastily retreated, though in perfectly good order. Nobody could quite say just what the trouble was. Emerson thought the men had been too "heady" and had fancied that "they too must assert and dogmatize." But one of Margaret's pupils declared that her erudition had quite outshone that of the men and even Mr. Emerson "had only served to display her powers." "His uncompromising idealism, his absolute denial of the fact of human nature," says this friend, "gave her opportunity and excite-

ment to unfold and illustrate her realism and acceptance of conditions." But even this loyal pupil has
one troubled after-thought: " I have thought sometimes that her acceptance of evil was *too great*." But
whether Margaret estranged the gentlemen by her
handling of evil or in some other way, they never came
again.

The oddest part of this affair was that Margaret
was all the while a prominent member of the Transcendental circle, where she was accepted on equal terms
by these same men. Among the Transcendentalists,
Margaret—as she said—" played the Mirabeau."
But here she was received as a woman who had " surpassed her sex," and her extraordinary conversational
gifts were warmly applauded. Perhaps she referred
to the Transcendental fraternity when she wrote:
" Their encomiums, indeed, are always in some sense
mortifying; they show too much surprise. ' Can this
be you?' he cries to the transfigured Cinderella; ' well,
I should never have thought it, but I am very glad.
. . . We will tell everyone that you have surpassed
your sex '." Margaret Fuller was far from being one
of those superior women who relish the distinction
of being " the only woman who."

In 1844, she published her *Woman in the Nineteenth Century.* It had previously appeared as an
essay in *The Dial* under the title of " The Great Law-

suit: Man versus Men; Woman versus Women."
But when the book was published, some of her friends
persuaded her to drop the cumbersome legalistic title
for the one she used. Margaret agreed reluctantly to
part with an unconscious but beloved souvenir of her
dead father's profession.

The only predecessor of Margaret's book was Mary
Wollstonecraft's *Vindication of the Rights of Woman*,
published fifty years before. The lives of these
two women had many circumstances in common.
Daughters of the middle class, poor-genteel, elder
sisters bearing the brunt of the burden of a large
family, spinsters of thirty-three—the same picture
applies to both when they published their feminist
books. In Mary's time, the doctrine of the abstract
rights of man engrossed the Paine-Godwin circle to
which she belonged, and Mary deduced from this her
theory of woman's rights. In Margaret's time,
natural rights had given way to socialism; Rousseau,
to Fourier. Margaret's circle talked of "attractive
industry" and the "liberty of law," and Margaret
applied these ideas to the position of her sex. "I
solicit of women," she says, "that they will lay it to
heart to ascertain what is for them the liberty of law.
It is for this, and not for any, the largest, extension
of partial privileges that I seek. I ask them, if interested in these suggestions, to search their own experi-

ences and intuitions for better, and fill up with fit materials the trenches that hedge them in." First and foremost she urged that women should be allowed to follow their natural bent in the choice of an occupation, and exclaimed enthusiastically, "Let them be sea-captains, if they will." This was her application of the principle of attractive industry to the woman's world in which she lived. Between her Dante, who compared Beatrice to an Admiral, and her Fourier, she derived no small encouragement for such bold images.

"I think women need," she wrote, "especially at this juncture, a much greater range of occupation than they have, to rouse their latent powers. . . . In families that I know, some little girls like to saw wood, others to use carpenter's tools. Where these tastes are indulged, cheerfulness and good humor are promoted. . . . Fourier had observed these wants of women, as no one can fail to do who watches the desires of little girls, or knows the ennui that haunts grown women, except where they make to themselves a serene little world by art of some kind. He, therefore, in proposing a great variety of employments, in manufactures or the care of plants and animals, allows for one-third of women as likely to have a taste for masculine pursuits, one-third of men for feminine. Who dares not observe the immediate glow and serenity that is diffused over the life of women, before restless or fretful, by engaging in gardening, building, or the lowest department of art? Here is something that is not routine, something that draws forth life towards the infinite."

To reassure those who shudder at a world in which all women would be converted into admirals, carpenters, and gardeners, Margaret goes on, " I have no doubt, however, that a large proportion of women would give themselves to the same employments as now, because there are circumstances that must lead them. Mothers will delight to make the nest soft and warm. Nature will take care of that." In another essay, she urged: " As you would not educate a soul to be an aristocrat, so do not to be a woman. A general regard to her usual sphere is dictated in the economy of nature. You need never enforce these provisions rigorously. Achilles had long plied the distaff as a princess; yet, at the first sight of a sword, he seized it. So with Woman; one hour of love would teach her more of her proper relations than all your formulas and conventions."

Examining Margaret's book in the light of present-day feminism, one cannot but be impressed by the comprehensiveness and enduring character of her views. " As the principle of liberty is better understood, and more nobly interpreted, a broader protest is made in behalf of Woman. As men become aware that few men have had a fair chance, they are inclined to say that no women have had a fair chance." In practice, she found, however, that this opinion was not general enough to prevent feminism from being a dangerous trade. "It demands some valor," she confessed, "to lift one's head amidst the shower of public squibs, private sneers, anger, scorn, derision, called out by the demand that women should be put on a par with their brethren, legally and politically; that they should hold property not by permission but by right, and that they should take an active part in all great movements."

She taught that women would have to win their own liberties. "I believe that, at present, women are the best helpers of one another. Let them think; let them act; till they know what they need. . . . I have urged on woman independence of man; not that I do not think the sexes mutually needed by one another, but because in woman this fact has led to an excessive devotion, which has cooled love, degraded marriage, and prevented either sex from being what it should be to itself or the other. . . . Man has gone but a little way; now he is waiting to see whether Woman can keep step with him; but instead of calling out, like a good brother, 'You can do it, if you only think so', or impersonally, 'anyone can do what he tries to do ', he often discourages, with schoolboy brag, ' Girls can't do that; girls can't play ball.' But let anyone defy their taunts, break through and be brave and secure, they rend the air with shouts. . . .

" Women are taught to learn their rule from without, not to unfold it from within. . . . The difficulty is to get them to the point from which they shall naturally develop self-respect and learn self-help. Once I thought that men would help to forward this state of things more than I do now. I saw so many of them wretched in the connections they had formed in weakness and vanity. They seemed so glad to esteem women whenever they could. . . . But early I perceived that men never, in any extreme of despair, wished to be women. . . . An intimate friend of the other sex said, in a fervent moment, that I ' deserved in some star to be a man.' He was much surprised when I disclosed my view of my position and hopes, when I declared my faith that the feminine side, the side of love, of beauty, of holiness, was now to have its full chance, and that, if either were better, it was better now to be a woman, for even the slightest achievement of good was an especial work of our time. He smiled incredulously. ' She makes the best she can of it,' thought he. ' Let Jews believe the pride of Jewry, but I am of the better sort, and know better.' . . . This by no means argues a willing want of generosity toward woman. Man is as generous toward her as he knows how to be."

She indignantly protested against one argument which has not disappeared even in our day. " Too much is said of women being better educated, that they may become better companions and mothers *for men.* . . . The intellect, no more than the sense of hearing, is to be cultivated merely that Woman may be a more valuable companion to Man, but because the Power who gave a power, by its mere existence signifies that it must be brought out toward perfection." . . . " Let it not be said, wherever there is energy of creative genius, ' She has a masculine mind '."

Margaret thought that the increase in the number of spinsters, though regrettable, might, after all, be the harbinger of better days. " In this regard of self-dependence, . . . we must hail as a preliminary the increase of the class contemptuously designated as ' old maids '. We cannot wonder at the aversion with which old bachelors and old maids have been regarded. . . . Those who have a more full experience of the instincts have a distrust as to whether the unmarried can be thoroughly human and humane." But, after all, this state of things she deemed to be the lesser of the two evils. " We shall not decline celibacy as the great fact of the time. It is one from which no vow, no arrangement, can at present save a thinking mind. For now the rowers are pausing on their oars; they wait a change before they can pull together. ! . . Union is only possible to those who are units."

Without any help from modern psychology, Margaret was most intelligently aware of the criss-crossing of the sexes by character-types which are common to both. "There is no wholly masculine man," she wrote, "no purely feminine woman. History jeers at the attempts of physiologists to bind great original laws by the forms which flow from them. They make a rule; they say from observation what can and cannot be. In vain! Nature provides exceptions to every rule. She sends women to battle, and sets Hercules spinning; she enables women to bear immense burdens, cold, and frost; she enables man, who feels maternal love, to nourish his infant like a mother. . . . Presently she will make a female Newton, and a male Siren. Man partakes of the feminine in the Apollo, Woman of the masculine as Minerva. . . .

"Let us be wise, and not impede the soul. Let her work as she will. Let us have but one creative energy, one incessant revelation. Let it take what form it will, and let us not bind it by the past to man or woman, black or white. Jove sprang from Rhea, Pallas from Jove. So let it be."

Margaret reminds her readers that women have never lacked for power, but it is the power that " vanity would crave " rather than that which " wisdom would accept." " It is not the transient breath of poetic incense that women want. . . . It is not life-long sway; it needs but to become a coquette, a shrew, or a good cook, to be sure of that. It is not money, nor notoriety, nor the badges of authority which men have appropriated to themselves. If demands made in their behalf lay stress on any of these particulars, those who make them have not searched deeply into the needs. . . . Ye cannot believe it, men; but the only reason why women ever assume what is more appropriate to you, is because you prevent them from finding out what is fit for themselves. Were they free, were they wise, fully to develop the strength and beauty of Woman, they would never wish to be men, or manlike."

Margaret could not forbear a few sarcastic comments on the subject of chivalry to women. " Men are very courteous to them. They praise them often; check them seldom. There is chivalry in the feeling towards ' the ladies,' which gives them the best seats in the stage-coach, frequent admission, not only to lectures of all sorts, but to courts of justice, halls of legislature, reform conventions. The newspaper editors ' would be better pleased that the *Lady's Book* should be filled up exclusively by ladies. It would then, indeed, be a true gem, worthy to be presented by young men to the mistress of their affections.' Can gallantry go further? "

Sometimes she feels that she must apologize for her aggressiveness. " If it has been the tendency of these remarks," she says, "to call Woman rather to the Minerva side, . . . let it be pardoned! It is love that has caused this, love for many incarcerated souls that might be freed, could the idea of religious self-dependence be established in them, could the weakening habit of dependence on others be broken up. . . . I would have Woman lay aside all thought, such as she habitually cherishes, of being taught and led by men. . . . Men do *not* look on both sides, and women must leave off asking them and being influenced by them, but retire within themselves, and explore the groundwork of life till they find their peculiar secret. . . .

"As to this living so entirely for men, I should think when it was proposed to women they would feel, at least, some spark of the old spirit of races allied to our own. 'If he is to be my bridegroom *and lord,*' cries Brunhilda, 'he must first be able to pass through fire and water.' . . . If women are to be bond-maids, let it be to men superior to women in fortitude, in aspiration, in moral power, in refined sense of beauty. You who give yourselves ' to be supported ' or because ' one must love something,' are they who make the lot of the sex such that mothers are sad when daughters are born."

Margaret did not hesitate to criticize the institution of marriage and discuss the evils of prostitution. One can imagine how the lavender window-panes of Boston must have trembled with the shock and how all the decent family people sitting tight behind the panes must have felt about this incorrigible woman and her unnecessary outspokenness. "Civilized Europe is still in a transition state about marriage," she wrote, "not only in practice, but in thought. It is idle to speak of the nations where polygamy is an institution, or seraglios a custom, while practices far more debasing haunt, well-nigh fill, every city and every town." She drew a comparison between the Christian citizen and the Oriental polygamist to show the superior morality of the latter. The Christian legislator, she says, declares that prostitution must be, it is a necessary accompaniment of civilization;—"he will and must buy the comforts and commercial advantages of his London, Vienna, Paris, New York, by conniving at the moral death, the damnation, so far as the action of society can insure it, of thousands of women for each splendid metropolis." But the Oriental, who had several wives and many hand-maidens, she considered, "did not wrong according to his light. What he did, he might publish it to God and man; it was not a wicked secret that hid in vile lurking-places and dens. . . . These women were not lost, not polluted in their own eyes, nor those of others." She denounced the marriage *de convenance,* which prevailed in her day, as little better than the Turkish slave-trade, though the Turkish slave, in that her situation was not "in defiance of an acknowl-edged law of right," was at least to this extent less degraded than the fashionable débutante. We find her always dwelling on this essential conflict in the Christian view of the erotic life.

But she was also practical. "Early marriages are desirable," she said, "but . . . the world is now so out of joint that there are a hundred thousand chances to one against it." How was the young man then (not even Margaret was bold enough to worry about young women) to lead "a virtuous and happy life?" Nowadays when social hygiene lecturers stump the country on this theme, and have withal a neat pre-scription for the difficult achievement, the subject has little novelty for us. But in Margaret's day, people did not talk about such things, and certainly no woman except herself would have had the courage. "Cold bathing and exercise will not suffice to keep a life pure," she advised young men, "without an inward baptism, and noble, exhilarating employment for the thoughts and passions." But in one respect, Margaret did not entirely fall into line with our most recent social hygienists. "Women are accustomed to be told by men that the reform is to come *from them.* 'You,' say the men, 'must frown upon vice; you must decline the attentions of the corrupt.' . . . This seems to us hard. Men have, indeed, been for more than a hundred years rating women for countenancing vice. But at the same time, they have carefully hid from them its nature, so that the preference often shown by women for bad men arises rather from a confused idea that they are bold and adventurous, acquainted with regions which women are forbidden to explore. . . . As to marriage, it has been inculcated in women for centuries, that men have not only stronger passions than they, but of a sort that it would be shameful for them to share or even understand." And yet, the indictment continues, "the least appearance of coldness or withdrawal, from whatever cause, in the wife is wicked, because liable to turn her husband's thoughts to illicit indulgence; for a man is so constituted that he must indulge his passions or die!"

Though Margaret's book did not dwell especially

on political rights, she emphatically included them. "Woman should have not only equal *power* with men," she wrote, "for of that omnipotent nature will never suffer her to be defrauded,—but a *chartered* power, too fully recognized to be abused. . . . Man should prove his own freedom by making her free. . . . Let him trust her entirely, and give her every privilege already acquired for himself,—elective franchise, tenure of property, liberty to speak in public assemblies, and so forth."

Margaret's little volume was the first considered statement of feminism in this country. It did not, as she said, argue for this or that particular privilege, but for an all-inclusive "woman's charter." Its fame spread rapidly. Her brother Eugene found people in New Orleans reading and discussing it and Jane Carlyle read it in Chelsea. In many respects it was more humane, less denunciatory, and less Puritan in temper than the Declaration of Sentiments, adopted a few years later. But Margaret's spirit and her breadth of view were carried over by this insurgent group which organized the woman's rights conventions of the early '50's. Women told on the platform of how they had read her book and, as they learned for the first time that there were other women with the same feelings as themselves, their "incarcerated souls" had been liberated. We have the story of how Susan B. Anthony went out to Mount Auburn one Saturday morning in 1855 and wandered about trying to find Margaret Fuller's monument but had to come away without finding it,—" which she regretted." Margaret was a vivid presence in these early years of the woman movement.

But as time went on and " woman's rights " narrowed down to a strictly suffrage basis, her name was more rarely heard. There were several reasons for this neglect. Margaret's plea was for the broadest possible development of women, for the realization of their destiny as human beings. Her philosophical feminism became indigestible for those engaged in the intense and single-minded propaganda for the ballot. She wanted elbow-room and scope,—claiming her emotional rights with the same conviction as her economic and political rights. In acting upon her beliefs, she did not escape the fatal " breath of scandal " and the consequent loss of a one hundred per cent respectability. This made her apologists uneasy and therefore prone to forget her. But as long as the generation of women who had known and loved her survived, she did not lack for sympathetic advocates with posterity. At last came a time, however, when the published reminiscences of her Transcendental friends formed the only portrait which remained. The personality which emerged from their memoirs is the contradictory and pretentious caricature which survives under the name of Margaret Fuller.

The truth is that the men who made the book about Margaret gave a better portrait of themselves in that volume than they did of its subject. For instance, they created a legend about her having a neck like a serpent, which she " would wind about and make as serpentine as possible." Several of them dwelt upon this serpentine association with great enthusiasm, and seemed to think it quite an original inspiration. Woman— wisdom—serpent:—it is a combination to which the long road of man's memory seems easily to lead. Horace Walpole could find no more satisfactory insult for Mary Wollstonecraft than to call her " a philosophizing serpent." The conscious memory of the Puritan is short, but his unconscious memory endureth forever.

Over against the voluminous reminiscences of the two-volume *Memoirs,* composed by her masculine contemporaries, so curiously lacking in any real feeling for the dead comrade, one would like to set the few friendly words of gentle Rebecca Spring, written half a century after Margaret's death. " For years afterwards, if I went to the seashore, I would dream of Margaret, always pleasantly. In my dream, she always seemed happy; it may be that the requiem of the winds and waves was the best for her. She believed in the higher education or women and in equal rights for them as citizens. She would have rejoiced in the wonderful progress they have made in these things since her time. Let our sex never forget Margaret Fuller."

CHAPTER VI

THE TRANSCENDENTALIST

EARLY in Margaret's Boston career, George Sand burst upon a startled world. Naturally Margaret followed her life and works with breathless interest, and envied the *femme libre* in her. And because she envied, she sometimes told herself that she had something which Sand had not, or that Sand had also failed where she had failed. " George Sand smokes, wears male attire, wishes to be addressed as *mon frère,*" she said; " perhaps, if she found those who *were* as brothers indeed she would not care whether she were brother or sister." Evidently Margaret was rather complacent at that time over her position in the Transcendental fellowship as compared with George Sand's place in her socialist circle. In the same provincial spirit, she wrote to Emerson that, so far as the real enigmas of life were concerned, " Sand and her friends seem to have solved [them] no better than M. F. and her friends." She was proud of her place among the Transcendentalists, where she wielded a lorgnette very much as George Sand used her cigarette—to vindicate the intellectual claims of her sex.

But time gradually weaned her away from the Transcendental view of life's enigmas towards a greater sympathy with George Sand's; in later years she learned there was a difference.

Margaret's connection with this eminent New England group is the part of her life to which we need give least attention here. It is the part which is best known and which has given her her textbook fame. The " American Literature " class, conning the pages under " Transcendentalism," always finds Margaret's name written there with that of Emerson and all the rest. High school classes nowadays may speak of these people with a pious regard—they are a sacred memory like the Boston tea-party—but they enjoyed no such respect from their own contemporaries. The opinion of John Quincy Adams was even tolerant by the side of the opinion of most. Adams explained their origin in this way: " A young man named Ralph Waldo Emerson, after failing in the everyday occupations of Unitarian preacher and schoolmaster, starts a new doctrine of Transcendentalism, declares all the old revelations superannuated and worn out, and announces the approach of new revelations and prophecies." This was the voice of the elders, condemning an upstart cult, and it was mild by comparison with that of the plain business man of Boston. " You know, *we* consider *those men* insane," one of them said

to Margaret.   They circulated stories about Emerson
going to a dinner party in top-boots, stories about
Margaret as a précieuse and Alcott as a maniac.   Margaret was fully identified with the group and whatever
ungraceful notoriety she had not earned through her
connection with the cause of woman's rights was now
hers through her connection with these Boston
" zanies," as one New Yorker politely called them.
The victims of the caricatures viewed their case with
commendable good humor.   " We are all a little wild
here," wrote Emerson to Carlyle, " with numberless
projects of social reform.   Not a reading man but
has a draft of a new community in his waistcoat
pocket.   I am gently mad myself, and am resolved
to live cleanly.   George Ripley is talking up a colony
of agriculturists and scholars, with whom he threatens
to take the field and the book.   One man renounces
the use of animal foods; and another of coin; and another of domestic hired service; and another of the
State; and on the whole we have a commendable share
of reason and hope."   But it was not the kind of
reason and hope that the " rooted capitalists "—as
Emerson called them—could share in as making for
a bigger and a better Boston.

The nickname of " Transcendentalist " stuck and
became historical.   It was a vulgarization of the Kan-
tian term, but as applied to this New England group

it meant practically nothing more than " Idealists ". But by its awkward and esoteric form, it obscured a great deal. It made the movement seem like a transient and isolated phenomenon of New England life instead of a part, as it was, of the spiritual revolution then sweeping over Europe. The young man named Ralph Waldo Emerson who announced the approach of new revelations and prophecies did not have to wait long until his announcements were thoroughly vindicated. A further obscurity produced by the foreign polysyllable was the simple fact that these people were liberals and socialists as the terms were understood and used in those days when there was scarcely a distinction between them. But Margaret's friends have not been commemorated under these political and economic classifications. Indeed, the word " liberal " has hardly existed in the American language since the death of Horace Greeley, with whom not only the name but the fact passed out of existence.

Transcendentalism, in brief, was a reaction against Puritan orthodoxy in every department of life,—politics, economics, religion, and education. Margaret Fuller reacted more strongly in certain directions than did her fellows; she revolted primarily against the æsthetic starvation and the kind of devil-worship which stamped the Puritan morality of her ancestors. Her explanation of Transcendentalism was this:

" Since the Revolution, there has been little, in the circumstances of this country, to call out the higher sentiments. The effect of continued prosperity is the same on nations as on individuals—it leaves the nobler faculties undeveloped. . . . New England is now old enough,—some there have leisure enough,—to look at all this, and the consequence is a violent reaction, in a small minority. . . . They see that political freedom does not necessarily produce liberality of mind, nor freedom in church institutions, vital religion; and, seeing that these changes cannot be wrought from without inwards, they are trying to quicken the soul, that they may work from within outwards. . . . Man is not made for society, but society is made for man. No institution can be good which does not tend to improve the individual. . . . I agree with those who think that no true philosophy will try to ignore or annihilate the material part of man, but will rather seek to put it in its place as servant and minister to the soul." This was Margaret's version of the Transcendentalist faith.

In 1840, Mr. George Ripley put his project of " field and book " into execution, and with the assistance of some friends established Brook Farm near Roxbury, Massachusetts. Margaret was urged to become a member of the community, but she could not be won for any project which involved living on a farm.

She went there often as a visitor but she would not be
a resident.   Mrs. George Ripley, whose learning was
as prodigious as her own, could spend her days con-
tentedly over the ironing-board in the Brook Farm
laundry.   But Margaret could not be induced to join
them even by the offer of " brain-work," like teach-
ing.   The bitterness of the combat with her father
about the Groton farm, from which she had emerged
as a remorseful victor, was probably the main reason
why she would never on any terms reside at Brook
Farm.   But among all her objections there was never
a hint that she had once tried farm-life and did not
like it.   Nothing so simple.   On the contrary, she
argued over Fourier upon whose theories and schemes
the place was founded.   She sympathized with the
heroism which prompted the experiment, but " in
judgment she considered it premature."   She thought
association the great experiment of the age, but still
only an experiment; to which the others replied that
they had no confidence in it beyond this.   " But they
seem to me to have," said Margaret stubbornly.   She
did not " agree with the principle of paying for services by time," but there were Brook Farmers themselves who sided with her on this point.   Then she
thought up another objection: " It is a constellation,
not a phalanx, to which I would belong."   Finally, she
could not subscribe to their system of ethics, for she

did not " believe in the hope of excluding evil, for that
was a growth of nature and one condition of the development of good." And here again she had only
to turn to Fourier himself to find abundant support,
for her theory of the instincts and passions was far
more in accordance with his own than were those of
the actual Brook Farmers. Higginson said of the
community, " There was a singular moral purity
about it which observers from the point of view of
Paris or even London have since found a little con-
temptible." Fourier might have been somewhat
surprised himself at the compromise theory there
achieved between his ideas and the most rigorous Puritan standards.

The association of Margaret Fuller's name with
that of Brook Farm rests chiefly on Hawthorne's
Blithedale Romance, in which he portrays the life
of the place and represents Margaret as its central
figure. Margaret's friends, who thought Zenobia
an unflattering portrait, based their defense on a
simple, literal alibi : as she had never lived at Brook
Farm, Zenobia could not have been meant for
her by the author, who really was a resident. But
this was merely an evasion of an uncomfortable fact.
One needs only to read Hawthorne's life and letters,
as published by his son, to realize that Zenobia was
certainly Hawthorne's version of Margaret Fuller and

that he had even less complimentary versions in his private note-books and journals. Through their publication, Hawthorne has come to be one of the chief contributors to Margaret's fame. Apparently their actual acquaintance was of the slightest; in fact Hawthorne was a solitary man who held himself aloof from the talkative Transcendentalists and especially aloof from the female of the species. Margaret was merely an idea to him, but withal a strangely engrossing idea. His obsessive interest in her personality has led to an artificial association of their names for which Margaret certainly was not responsible. Her attentions were all frankly focused on Mr. Emerson.

We can only understand Hawthorne's excessive antagonism by taking a look at his own mental patterns. Once when invited to dine at Mr. Bancroft's with her, he wrote in his note-book, " Providence had given me some other business to do for which I was very thankful." According to his own reminiscences, he had but recently escaped from the clutches of a certain " nefarious female," very much like Margaret, who, merely to gratify her own vanity, had induced him to challenge a friend to a duel. Happily, the duel was avoided by the discovery of the lady's base character, whereupon—says the biography —" Hawthorne went to Mary and crushed her." His excessive self-righteousness and his abnormal fear of women were symptoms of a mental distress which bordered on the pathological. When he at last became engaged in his late thirties, he postponed his marriage for several years on the ground that the news would kill his mother. "While I love you so dearly, . . ." he wrote to his fiancée, "still I have an awe of you that I never felt for anybody else." A young man in this state of mind naturally postpones his wedding day. His biography is full of morbid symptoms of a malady which grew upon him with advancing years and weakened his mental powers long before his comparatively early death. His violent repugnance to the nude statues which he saw in Italy, his intemperate tirade against a painted Venus, and his attack on Margaret's character written in his note-books at this time, all indicated a mental *malaise* which had grown all but unbearable. Like many gentle, suffering souls he was capable of the deepest malice; and his life-long preoccupation with the concepts of sin and guilt,— the central theme of all his novels,—made a healthy outlook on the facts of life increasingly impossible. His immoderate dislike of Margaret is only comprehensible as a symptom of his hidden misery, a cover for his fascinated interest in a Bacchante type. Yet even an amiable critic like Henry James took Hawthorne's antagonism seriously, and recorded it as a bad mark against Margaret's personality. One of the most recent biographers of Hawthorne justifies his view of Margaret by declaring that " she was a revolutionary character, a sort of female Garibaldi, who attacked old Puritan traditions with a two-edged sword. She won victories for liberalism and socialism, but she left confusion behind her." The portrait, by no means an unjust one, explains, as the author intends it to explain, why Hawthorne did not like Margaret Fuller; but it does not explain why, for all his distaste, he simply could not leave her alone. The reason for that lay deep within himself. No doubt he received the same sort of emotional satisfaction from vilifying her that his near ancestor had received from whipping a witch through the streets of Salem. This complexity of feeling expressed itself more freely and truly through his art, for the wicked Zenobia was by no means lacking in attractiveness and charm.

As already said, Margaret's actual encounters with Hawthorne appear to have been few and trivial, and, by her, entirely unnoted. But his references to them magnify their importance. Once she wrote a note to Hawthorne's wife, inquiring whether her newly married sister and brother-in-law might come to board with the Hawthornes at Concord. Hawthorne insisted on answering the letter himself, though it had been addressed to his wife, on the chivalrous pre-

university out of our straws," he wrote to Margaret, and after outlining the courses, he invited her to join the " puissant faculty " which would " front the world without charter, diploma, corporation, or steward." The university never came off, but *The Dial* did; that is to say, it came off after a fashion, though it threatened to fall through with every issue. Without Margaret's executive talents, it certainly would not have lasted as long as it did. During the first two years of the quarterly, she was editor-in-chief; and when she resigned, Emerson assumed the editorship-in-chief for another two years. Still Margaret continued as associate editor and contributor, and *The Dial* did not finally give up the ghost until she left Boston for New York. It was succeeded, in effect, by *The Harbinger,* published by the Brook Farm phalanx with George Ripley as editor. *The Harbinger,* to which Margaret was an occasional contributor, was specifically devoted to socialistic propaganda, and lasted, like *The Dial,* for a term of four years. Its editor later succeeded to Margaret Fuller's place as literary critic of the *New York Tribune.*

The Dial was, from its beginning, chiefly the expression of the personalities of Margaret Fuller and Emerson. The initial number of this journal of the new spirit began with a leader by Emerson and an *Essay on Critics* by Margaret. " No one can converse much with different classes of society in New England," wrote Emerson, "without remarking the progress of a revolution. Those who share in it have no external organization, no badge, no creed, no name. . . . It is in every form a protest against usage, and a search for principles. In all its movements, it is peaceable, and in the very lowest marked with a triumphant success. . . . It has the step of Fate, and goes on existing like an oak or a river, because it must." Margaret's essay which followed Emerson's contained her view of a literary craft of which she was, and still remains, one of the most distinguished representatives in this country. "The critic is beneath the maker, but is his needed friend," she wrote. "The critic is not a base caviler, but the younger brother of genius. Next to invention is the power of interpreting invention; next to beauty the power of appreciating beauty. And of making others appreciate it; for the universe is a scale of infinite gradation, and below the very highest, every step is explanation down to the lowest. . . . Nature is the literature and art of the divine mind; human literature and art the criticism on that; and they, too, find their criticism within their own sphere." Real critics, she said, would not write as guide-books or expurgatory indexes but as companions and friends. "We would live with them, rather than be taught by them how to live; we would catch the contatagion of their mental activity, rather than have them direct us how to regulate our own."

Margaret was to have been paid two hundred dollars a year for her work as editor. But *The Dial* never prospered sufficiently to pay even this one small salary. How Margaret must have labored with her unpaid contributors is not hard to imagine. " My vivacious friend," as Emerson called her, had to call up all her reserves of vivacity to keep her columns filled. "Henry, I adjure you in the name of all the Genii, Muses, Pegasus, Apollo, Pollio, Apollyon," she wrote to Henry Hedge in Bangor, " to send me something good for this journal, before the first of May. All mortals, my friend, are slack and bare; they wait to see whether Hotspur wins, before they levy aid for as good a plan as ever was laid. I know you are plagued and it is hard to write; just so it is with me, for I also am a father." Oftener than she liked Margaret was compelled to fill in with her own compositions, for she was not over-proud of them. " In truth I have not much to say," she declared, " for since I have had leisure to look at myself, I find that, so far from being an original genius, I have not yet learned to think to any depth, and that the utmost I have done in life has been to form my character to a certain consistency, cultivate my tastes, and learn to tell the truth with a little better grace than I did at first." There is certainly very little of the "mountainous me" in this sort of self-criticism, of which there are many instances in Margaret's diaries.

The common criticism was that *The Dial* was too "feminine." Carlyle protested irritably that the journal was "no stalwart Yankee *man* with color in the cheeks of him, and a coat on his back." It was true that the editor wore a shawl, and one suspects that this fact had something to do with the impression of femininity ascribed to the whole enterprise. Theodore Parker, who was one of the chief contributors and quite stalwart and masculine, also thought that what *The Dial* needed was a beard. He accordingly established a quarterly of his own, after the failure of *The Dial,* which undertook to give the public its beard. But he prospered no better than his predecessor, his journal turning out—to quote Mr. Higginson's little joke—"to be the beard without *The Dial.*"

The story of *The Dial's* rise and fall is linked with the story of Emerson's and Margaret's friendship. Emerson was a man of many friendships; having severed relations with Church and State, he reserved his loyalties for individual affiliations. His classic friendships were with Carlyle and Margaret Fuller; Carlyle he had chosen, but Margaret had chosen him. After her father's death, Margaret re-

solved to have Emerson for her guide and mentor
and had set out to win him. " Margaret, who had
stuffed me out as a philosopher in her own fancy,"
reads Emerson's account, " was too intent on estab-
lishing a good footing between us, to omit any art of
winning." But it was only after a long resistance and
then not very gracefully that he yielded. " Of course,
it was impossible long to hold out against such urgent
assault," he remarks. In spite of this inauspicious
beginning, the friendship went better later on.
Emerson said that, during an intimacy which lasted
for ten years, he never saw her without surprise at
her new powers. He carefully preserved every letter
that she wrote him and included her in his various
schemes. But all the while he feared her temperament, much as Goethe feared Beethoven's. " Such
people pull down the pillars of the temple," said
Goethe of Beethoven; " I . . . had a feeling as if a
voice cried, *Stand from under,*" said Emerson of
Margaret. Emerson feared for his unshakable calm
in the presence of the ardor and abandon of his friend.
" It was a war of temperaments," he said; but added
that " the incongruity never interrupted for a moment
the intercourse, such as it was, that existed between
us."

But the ardent disciple in time became a critic, not
a critic of details but a questioner of the foundation-

stone of Emerson's whole existence. She could not give her sanction to his cloistered life in Concord; for herself, she told him, she preferred "the animating influences of Discord." And to a friend she wrote, "What did you mean by saying that I had imbibed much of his way of thought? I do indeed feel his life stealing gradually into mine; and I sometimes think that my work would have been more simple, and my unfolding to a temporal activity more rapid and easy, if we had never met." Again she wrote, "Leave him in his cell affirming absolute truth; protesting against humanity, if so he appears to do; the calm observer of the courses of things." In Margaret the force of Puritan tradition was fast wearing away; she had hovered for long between Goethe and Emerson and Goethe had in the end prevailed.

No doubt they rather liked their arguments, into which they seemed to fall so naturally and so irreconcilably. To please Margaret's memories, Emerson had to go on fighting the departed Timothy's battles over and over again; and to please Emerson, Margaret had to go on playing the part of his obstructive Aunt Mary Moody Emerson. This Calvinistic maiden aunt, who had taken the place of Emerson's dead father, was a woman of unusual force of character, enormous learning, and great outspokenness. It is not to be wondered at if Emerson could not forbear getting back at the tyrannical "auntism" of his Transcendental colleague from time to time. Nor is it surprising that he could maintain his attitude of resistance within a friendship which he apparently had no wish to break away from. He wrote a character portrait of his aunt after her death which contained some striking points of similarity with his memoir of Margaret. Were the older and the younger women really so much alike or did he unconsciously tend to force them both into a single cherished mold? Probably he liked his second maiden aunt and her Platonic attentions better than he ever admitted to himself.

Margaret abandoned her career of hermitism and mysticism in 1843, and tried traveling instead. She journeyed by way of the Great Lakes to Chicago, and spent the summer in a survey of the Far West. She traveled in an ox wagon over the grassy plains of Illinois and penetrated into the territory of Wisconsin. The Indians still dwelt in scattered encampments while German and Swedish immigrants were daily disembarking at the Chicago piers. She ate white-fish in Chicago, weighed the Indians' cause, and visited in log-cabin homes along the Rock River. There is certainly little suggestion of frailty and invalidism in the following description of an over-night stop at Ross's Grove: "We ladies were to sleep in the bar-room,

from which its drinking visitors could be ejected only
at a late hour. . . . We had also rather hard
couches (mine was the supper table) but we Yankees
born to rove, were altogether too much fatigued to
stand upon trifles, and slept as sweetly as we would
in the 'bigly bower' of any baroness. But I think
England [referring to an English lady of the party]
sat up all night, wrapped in her blanket shawl, with
a neat lace cap upon her head, so that she would have
looked perfectly the lady, if anyone had come in.
. . . She watched, as her parent country watches
the seas, that nobody may do wrong in any case, and
deserved to have met some interruption, she was so
well prepared."

Margaret returned home and described her western
travels in a little volume entitled, *Summer on the
Lakes*. The book made but little impression but it
had at least one appreciative reader in Mr. Horace
Greeley. The West was his hobby, and here was a
woman who had caught the idea. " Wherever the hog
comes, the rattlesnake disappears," wrote Margaret
with some of Mr. Greeley's own tang. Mrs. Greeley
was already an admirer of Margaret's, having attended
the Conversations during her visits in Boston. It
was she who set the plans on foot for having Margaret on the *Tribune* staff—and at the same time a
resident in the Greeley home.

Margaret was delighted with the prospect of becoming a journalist in New York. But Mr. Emerson did not approve of the step, and retained his disapproval even though the venture obviously turned out so well. He wrote to Carlyle two years later, "Margaret Fuller's work as critic of all new books, critic of the drama, of music, and good arts in New York, has been honorable to her. Still this employment is not satisfactory to me." And though Margaret said the circulation of the *Tribune* was 50,000, Emerson mentioned it in this letter to Carlyle as but 30,000. Some natural resentment may have been felt over the loss of a maiden aunt and right-hand man in one.

CHAPTER VII

THE JOURNALIST

THE *New York Tribune* was in the fourth year of its existence when Margaret Fuller became a member of the staff. In those days, Horace Greeley was the *Tribune* and the *Tribune* was Horace Greeley; the man and his journal were one.

In all his personal relations, the editor was amiable and good-natured to a fault, but he was one of the most passionate political campaigners and election warriors that American history has produced. Once a political antagonist in Washington who did not know him personally, struck him with a horsewhip; even rival editors were incensed by the assault and one of them said that "the fellow who would strike Horace Greeley would strike his mother." The *Tribune* was like its editor, incessantly campaigning, reforming, and crusading and yet exceedingly popular and prosperous. Though Mr. Greeley came of Puritan stock, he had the saving graces of his Irish blood.

As Margaret was a woman's woman, Mr. Greeley was a man's man. His real home was in his newspaper office and his real life was lived there with his host of friends. He was the center of a group of persons engrossed with the labor problem and the social reforms of the day. Important figures of this circle were William H. Channing, the minister; Marcus Spring, the merchant; Albert Brisbane, the wealthy scholar; and the silent Mr. McElrath, who was Mr. Greeley's business partner. They all co-operated in various ways with Mr. Greeley's schemes for the emancipation of labor. William Channing was a preacher and a kind of social reformer-at-large. He and Margaret Fuller together made a survey of New York's philanthropic institutions in order that Margaret might write up her observations for the *Tribune.* Marcus Spring, like Horace Greeley, was an ardent supporter of the North American phalanx at Red Bank, New Jersey. Albert Brisbane expounded the ideas of Fourier, the prophet of the social revolution, on the front page of the *Tribune,* and Margaret fell heir to this space when he left for Europe in 1845. Most important of them all, perhaps, was the faithful Mr. McElrath who kept the *Tribune's* house in order and maintained a perfect organization in spite of the picturesque and incorrigible disorder of the chief. "As Damon and Pythias are the types of perfect friendship," exclaims Greeley's biographer, "so may Greeley and McElrath be of a perfect partnership; and we may say, with a sigh at the many discordant unions the world presents, oh! that every Greeley could find his McElrath and blessed is the McElrath that finds his Greeley!" Mr. Greeley's coterie embraced all sorts and conditions of men, until life in the editorial offices seemed to be one never-ending stag-party.

Mrs. Greeley apparently felt the need of a friend—her husband had so many. She was often lonely and dejected and there was a lack of "mental harmony", —so Margaret said,—in the domestic atmosphere. Wives like Mrs. Greeley and Xantippe really have a case, though their genial and convivial husbands usually get all the sympathy. Mrs. Greeley was probably trying to find *her* McElrath when she invited Margaret Fuller to share her home. Mr. Greeley said that he regarded Margaret as his wife's friend rather than his own, and added ungraciously that he could not understand the adoring women friends who flocked out to his home to see her. Perhaps it was but natural under the circumstances that he should look on his wife's friend and her numerous disciples with rather a critical and distrustful eye. It was too much like having the tables suddenly turned on himself. Margaret's book on the woman question had "made quite a breeze," as Mrs. Peabody, who kept a bookstore in Boston, said in describing its success. This fact must have greatly increased the number of Margaret's visitors and stirred up more interest in feminism within the Greeley home than the editor himself could comfortably subscribe to.

Still the business partnership between Margaret and her chief was a most successful one. Mr. Greeley had the profoundest respect for his literary critic and considered her "the best instructed woman in America;" while Margaret had the highest regard for the editor's great abilities and his generous disposition as an employer. Mr. Greeley knew more about the labor problem than any American public man of his day, and Margaret acquired a groundwork in economics while she worked for the *Tribune* which served her well in the European whirlpool of revolution later. The editor was a hard beleaguered man, especially in the years of Margaret's association with his paper, and she was immovably on his side against the ruling classes. But at home, she was on the side of Mrs. Greeley.

Horace Greeley declared himself the friend of the woman movement. And so he was, but with important reservations. The kind of woman movement which he favored was purely for political and economic rights. It would never seek to reform the institution of marriage in any way; it would abolish divorce entirely; and it would never push its claim for suffrage at a time which the editor of the *Tribune* did not think propitious. But this was not the kind of woman movement which Margaret Fuller believed in and wrote about and Susan B. Anthony fought for. There were inevitable clashes of opinion between these women and a man who believed in the Episcopal marriage ceremony and the Roman Catholic attitude towards divorce. Though his religious views were so liberal that he belonged to a Universalist church, defended Tom Paine in his newspaper, and was denounced as an atheist by his enemies, he would be married by the Episcopal ceremony and no other and believed that the marriage tie should be absolutely indissoluble. Mrs. Greeley had a tendency to agree with Margaret Fuller, and later with Susan B. Anthony, rather than with her husband, on questions concerning women, which naturally did not increase her husband's sympathy with these rival influences.

His own account of his behavior as a host shows that Margaret must have been rather broad-minded to keep their relations as friendly as they were. He lectured her on her tea-drinking habits, telling her that this was the source of her ill-health and she should give it up at once. Also at every opportunity he pointed out her personal inconsistencies as a champion of the emancipated woman. If she demanded, as she did, free access to the professions, politics, and employments of the rougher sex, he said, she should not accept their protection as escorts. He also thought that, as a strong-minded woman, she should not give in so much to her headaches and " spinal affliction " and boasted that he could write ten columns to her one a day. In the old *Dial* days, Emerson had regarded her as a marvel of speed. Lucky for Mr. Emerson, he did not work for Mr. Greeley. And did not Mr. Greeley himself have boils, was he not covered with them like Job, and did he not do a day's work every day regardless of his sufferings? Incidentally, it does not appear that Margaret failed to live up to her contract of three articles a week, but what was this to the hero of ten thousand paragraphs? The point was that she could not keep up with him, and this was a point which Mr. Greeley never failed to make. He cared for nothing in life so much as just winning; when a little boy, he cried if he lost the spelling-match and when he made the race for president, he could not survive the tragedy of his defeat. All this was because Horace Greeley had to make up for a father who had been a failure in life. The paternal Greeley had been an unsuccessful farmer and frontiersman, with a wife who could work as hard and drink as hard as he could himself. The mother of Horace Greeley, one learns from his biography,

" had the strength of a man without his coarseness," and she could out-rake any man in the town and load the hay-wagons as fast as her husband. The son of this Amazon refused to pay tribute to Margaret's prowess as an intellectual worker, however much others might be impressed by it.

During her career as a journalist in New York,— her business life, as she called it,—Margaret accomplished two definite things. She established herself as a leading American literary critic. The *Cambridge History of American Literature* describes her as " one of the best-equipped, most sympathetic, and genuinely philosophical critics produced in America prior to 1850." The second achievement of her New York career was a love affair.

This innocent and bourgeois romance was sedulously concealed for a long time by means of outright lying on the part of gallant Christian gentlemen. The painful, the unmentionable fact was that Margaret's hopes were disappointed; she was jilted, in short. But after fifty years or more the whole story came out through the publication of the *Love Letters of Margaret Fuller* with a preface by the faithless lover himself. The preface, dated 1873, shows that he prepared the letters for publication thirty years before they actually appeared; but for some reason, probably the interposition of a hand much stronger than his own, the letters remained unpublished until 1903. The poor man never saw this handsome tribute to himself in print. His reason for publishing Margaret's letters, he said, was to show "that great and gifted as she was as a writer, she was no less so in the soft and tender emotions of a true woman's heart."

The Greeley homestead, on the bank of the East River and at the foot of what is now Forty-ninth Street, was a favorable background for a summer romance. The place had been a summer residence, but Mr. Greeley dubbed it "The Farm" as he always insisted on viewing himself as a farmer. It was charmingly sequestered; a long lane connected it with the hourly stage on Third Avenue, while the windows overlooked, in the opposite direction, a scene of wide waters and moving sails. While Mr. Greeley cherished a day-dream of being a farmer, Margaret cherished one of going to sea, and both of them were delighted with the new home. The housekeeping went on "in Castle Rackrent style," for, unfortunately, the orderly sway of Mr. McElrath did not extend as far as The Farm. Margaret soon found, she said, that "things would not stay put" and gave up trying to better them. But there were eight acres of wooded grounds, a dell with falling water, paths that wound through myrtle and white cherry, and waves murmuring in the moonlight at the base of the rocks. It was an

ideal place in which to fall in love in the springtime.

Mr. James Nathan was a Jew from Hamburg, who
was engaged in the banking business in Wall Street.
When he was about forty-five, he changed his name
to Gotendorf, the name of a place in Holstein owned
by his father. He says that he did this by Horace
Greeley's advice, who also no doubt facilitated the act
of Congress by which the change of name was made
possible. Mr. Greeley would have taken any amount
of trouble on behalf of a man who strove, if only
symbolically, to regain the parental homestead. He
himself spent a lifetime regaining the lost paradise of
a Vermont farm which was wrested from his father
for debt when Horace was nine years old. " We de-
vote most of the excess of energy of maturity working out the wishes of childhood," says a modern
psychologist, so that perhaps Mr. Greeley's course
should not be looked upon as very exceptional, after
all. Certainly he spent a great deal of his mature
energies in the vicarious working out of those same
childish wishes.

When Mr. Gotendorf visited the Greeley Farm
he was still Mr. Nathan. About the same age as Margaret, he was a gentle, blue-eyed dreamer, who played
the guitar, wrote verses, and chafed at the uncongenial life of a business man. " I have long had a

presentiment," Margaret wrote to him, "that I should meet—nearly—one of your race, who would show me how the sun of today shines upon the ancient Temple —but I did not expect so gentle and civilized an apparition and with blue eyes!" Mr. James Nathan was not by temperament a man of action and was discontented with the lot which a masculine nature is supposed to crave; while Margaret, being emphatically a woman of action, had always struggled against the pressure of social customs which refused her any outlet for her energies. "We parted in the lane and went our opposite ways," said óne of Margaret's letters to her lover, "and I thought: my brother wishes to make his existence more poetic, I need mine should be more deeply real; must we go opposite ways in the same road?" More than once in her letters she refers to the "feminine sweetness and sensibility" of her lover's disposition.

Mr. Nathan suddenly departed from New York in June, 1845. He left his dog and his guitar in Margaret's care, and set forth upon long journeys through Europe and Palestine. His leaving has the air of a rather ungallant flight. He continued to send back travel articles to Margaret for publication in the *Tribune,* but his personal letters to her dwindled away. In the meantime Margaret's plans for a European trip had rapidly matured. She wrote to Mr.

Nathan, who had now retired to Hamburg and the protection of his mother, that she would be in London on September the first and hoped to see him then. Furthermore, her party would go from London to Hamburg along the usual route. One can imagine the sensations of the unhappy Mr. Nathan, who had become engaged to be married in the meantime but had forgotten to mention it when he wrote to Margaret and asked her to find a publisher for his book of travels. But the moment for candor had come. He rose to the heights of a man of action and dispatched a letter to Margaret in England which had the desired effect. It completely changed her itinerary. Mr. Nathan describes the episode in his preface twenty years after, —" She, in London, found letters, and then went to Rome and to Heaven, but the mutually much longed for meeting is yet to be, somewhere, somehow!"

The letters which Margaret found in London are referred to in her Journal: "From 1st June, 1845, to 1st Sept., 1846, a mighty change has taken place, I ween. I understand more and more the character of the *tribes*. I shall write a sketch of it and turn the whole to account in a literary way, since the affections and ideal hopes are so unproductive. I care not. I am resolved to take such disappointments more lightly than I have."

A few days later, she was lost on a lonely mountaintop in Scotland, where she spent a night of dangerous exposure. She wrote a letter to the *Tribune* describing her vigil, telling how she kept herself in motion the whole night long, while death seemed to woo her in visionary shapes. " Floating slowly and gracefully, their white robes would unfurl from the great body of mist in which they had been engaged, and come upon me with a kiss pervasively cold as that of death. What they might have told me, who knows, if I had but resigned myself more passively to that cold, spirit-like breathing! " The temptation to resign herself—though perhaps unconscious—was evidently strong upon her. But as it turned out, her uncomfortable night had the happy effect of curing the worst pangs of her disappointment, for she apparently forgot the faithless Mr. Nathan very soon. It was a desperate remedy like that of poor Mary Wollstonecraft whose plunge into the cold waters of the Thames seemed to do more than anything else to cure her of her hopeless love for the elusive Gilbert Imlay. It was true of both these ardent women that they were capable of consoling their orphaned affections by a rather sudden and complete transference to another and a different object.

But in spite of Mr. Nathan's heart-breaking desertion, he and his dog and his guitar probably helped to make Margaret into a better woman and a better critic. When she was in Italy, she was said to be quite humanized; and no doubt the emotional, blue-eyed foreigner was a happy antidote for the transcendental life just left behind in Boston. At any rate, her critical work on the *Tribune* shows a mind much more tempered to reality and purged of fantasy than the extracts in the *Memoirs* would lead one to expect. She was moving at last in a world of fact.

The *Tribune* was noted for the excellence and freedom of its reviews. Margaret had the task of reviewing the works of Carlyle, Browning, Elizabeth Barrett, and Tennyson as they first came from the press; while volumes by American contemporaries like Longfellow, Poe, and Lowell fell into her hands for judgment and appraisal. Her reviews were collected and published in a small volume entitled *Papers on Literature and Art,* which was read with appreciation in England and led to the offer of journalistic opportunities in London. As her previous books had promoted her transfer to New York, her critical papers would have given her a foothold among London journalists, had she been eager to gain one. Her strange indifference to these English offers was a part of her general lack of sympathy for England. She turned her back on London where she might perhaps have earned her bread with considerable distinction and embraced a life of pauperism in her beloved Italy.

A glance through Margaret's critical papers shows the strong, resonant fiber of her mind and an energy of character which is usually called masculine. She had little mercy for sentimentalisms of any kind. To a lady who over-modestly apologized for publishing, Margaret recommended that she "leave such affectations to her aunts; they were the fashion of their day." "Literature has become not merely an archive for the preservation of great thoughts, but a means of general communication between all classes of minds, and all grades of culture. There needs be no great fuss about publishing or not publishing. Those who forbear may rather be considered the vain ones, who wish to be distinguished among the crowd." In a review of the biography of Sir James Mackintosh, she analyzed him as a day-dreamer. "A man who means to think and write a great deal, must, after six and twenty, learn to read with his fingers." And she concluded from the character of this man that "man may escape from every foe and every difficulty, except what are within—himself." Reviewing Emerson, she says, "Here is, undoubtedly, the man of ideas; but we want the ideal man also—want the heart and genius of human life to interpret it. . . . We doubt this friend raised himself too early to the perpendicular, and did not lie along the ground long enough to hear the whispers of our parent life. We would wish he might be thrown by conflicts on the lap of mother earth, to see if he would not rise again with added powers." She had a very practical view of the uses of biography. " Both as physiological and psychical histories, they are full of instruction. . . . Let the physician compare the furies of Alfieri with the silent rages of Byron, and give the mother and pedagogue the light in which they are now wholly wanting, showing how to treat such noble plants in the early stages of growth."

Reviewing American literature in those days, when it was still so young and sensitive and a narrow patriotism was ever on the defensive, was a dangerous trade. Horace Greeley had found it so and Margaret also won her scars as a critic. On the whole Margaret's punishment was more severe. When Greeley was sued for libel by Fenimore Cooper and condemned to pay the author damages, the irrepressible editor at least enjoyed the comedy. " Fenimore shall have his $200," he assured the public; " we are glad to do anything for one of the most creditable (of old) of our authors." This famous suit had taken place but a short while before Margaret joined the *Tribune* staff. When Mr. Greeley gave into her hands the full critical sway of the most influential newspaper in America, he resigned a dangerous post which required courage as well as judgment in the holder. But Margaret was as honest as Mr. Greeley himself and had no more respect for the ruling classes; she was therefore as much as he bound to commit *lésé majesté* sooner or later. One day Mr. Greeley brought home a new volume by Longfellow for her to review. Margaret tried to put it off on the editor, saying that her view of poetry was so very different from that of Mr. Longfellow, who had grown by this time to be the most important American poet. Mr. Greeley at first consented to write the review himself, but then he said he had no time and Margaret had to write it after all. It is an easy guess that if he had been an admirer of Longfellow's he would have found time to write the more favorable criticism. His opinion probably differed but little from Margaret's, for Mr. Higginson tells us that Margaret's opinion of Longfellow and of Lowell as well, was commonly held among the Transcendentalists and was not merely a personal prejudice of hers.

"When we see a person of moderate powers," she wrote, "receive honors which should be reserved for the highest, we feel somewhat like assailing him and taking from him the crown which should be reserved for grander brows. And yet this is, perhaps, ungenerous. . . . He [Longfellow] has no style of his own, growing out of his own experiences and observations of nature. Nature with him, whether human

or external, is always seen through the windows of
literature. . . . This want of the free breath of
nature, this perpetual borrowing of imagery, this excessive, because superficial, culture which he has derived from an acquaintance with the elegant literature
of many nations and men, out of proportion to the
experience of life within himself, prevent Mr. Longfellow's verses from ever being a true refreshment to
ourselves."

Longfellow

But this was not the whole of her offending. She
thought Lowell's work of less worth than Longfellow's. "We cannot say as much for Lowell, who,
we must declare it, though to the grief of some friends
and the disgust of more, is absolutely wanting in the
true spirit and tone of poesy. His interest in the
moral questions of the day has supplied the want of
vitality in himself; his great facility at versification
has enabled him to fill the ear with a copious stream
of pleasant sound. But his verse is stereotyped; his
thought sounds no depth, and posterity will not remember him."

Lowell

Longfellow, famous for his amiability, passed over
the episode in silence and vindicated his reputation
for a sweet temper. But Lowell pursued Margaret in
public and private with bitter reprisals. He lam-
pooned her in his *Fable for Critics* as Miranda with
a ferocity which certainly should have relieved his

feelings and wiped out the score. But apparently his resentment was still unappeased, and he continued to pour it out in his private correspondence. Writing to William Story in Rome, he devotes most of his letter to Margaret. "I have it on good authority,"—he begins a long-drawn joke, "that the Austrian government has its eye on Miss F. It would be a pity to have so much worth and genius shut up for life in Spielberg. Her beauty might perhaps save her. Pio Nono also regards her with a naturally jealous eye, fearing that the college of cardinals may make her the successor of Pope Joan." In this strain, the joke continues and recurs throughout the letter until one quite agrees with Henry James's comment,—that Lowell's absorption in his joke is rather "a significant mark for Miss F."

When Margaret went to Europe, her connection with the *Tribune* remained unbroken. Her letters appeared on the front page of the newspaper, for she wrote as a foreign correspondent. In the meantime, soon after her departure, an important change had taken place in the editorial policy. Mr. Greeley had eliminated the theories of Fourier (at least under that name) from the columns of his paper. It had happened in this way.

Mr. Greeley had challenged Mr. H. J. Raymond of the *Courier and Enquirer* to a debate on socialism and

Fourierism, and Mr. Raymond had accepted. This was one of the occasions when Mr. Greeley's passion for debates and contests was his undoing. As long as he could keep the argument on property and poverty, capital and labor, Mr. Greeley was in his element, hitting hard and scoring vigorously. But Mr. Raymond, who was astute and a good Presbyterian, kept shifting the theme to marriage and family life in spite of his adversary's efforts to stick to capital and labor. Mr. Raymond quoted shocking things from Fourier, who had clearly never had the advantages of a New England education and who held that the passions are good in themselves,—that evil flows only from their repression or subversion. Poor Mr. Greeley hastened to " deny with disgust and indignation that there was in socialism, as American socialists understand and teach it, any provision or license for the gratification of criminal passions or unlawful desires." Mr. Raymond pursued his advantage and wrote solemn warnings against a social scheme which was in favor of " Bacchantes, Aspasias, and Bayardères " and declared that the *Tribune,* perhaps unknowingly, was helping to introduce such horrors into our midst. All of Mr. Greeley's protestations could not wipe out the stain thus cast upon his economic prophet, whose name was henceforth associated in the public mind with sexual immorality. The *Tribune* no longer dared to advocate even the economics of Fourier. Mr. Raymond had destroyed the menace. He was victor —and on this rock he founded the *New York Times*.

Now there was no one who had less desire than Mr. Greeley to stand up as the defender of " Bacchantes, Aspasias, and Bayardères," but fate and Mr. Raymond combined to force him into a position which his very soul repudiated. After the debate was over, and while Mr. Greeley was still trying to pretend to himself that he had not lost it, there came a staggering piece of news from Italy. It was reported that the lady correspondent of the *New York Tribune* had entered upon a sort of Fourieristic marriage in Rome. The awful consequences of the socialism of the *Tribune* stood revealed.

CHAPTER VIII

CONTACTS

THE friends with whom Margaret finally went to
Europe were Marcus and Rebecca Spring and their
little boy Edward. The Springs were apparently
fairy god-parents to many idealistic protégées. They
rescued Channing from an uncongenial life in the
West and provided a career for him in New York.
They took Fredrika Bremer to see New England; and
when Fredrika froze in the icy bed-chamber of a
Puritan farmhouse, they made up a bed for her before
the parlor fire and occupied the frigid guest-chamber
themselves. They took Margaret Fuller to see
Europe; and when Margaret was lost on the moun-
tain-top and the Scotch shepherds spent the night
looking for her, Mr. Spring gave them a splendid
party in return. Judged by their behavior toward
these friends, the Springs set little store by the virtues
of self-denial and took a naïve pleasure in giving
people what they wanted. The stoical Emerson said,
"The mind is its own place," but the kind-hearted
Springs thought that, when Channing was discontented with Cincinnati and Margaret Fuller consumed

by a desire to go to Europe, something ought to be done about it. The fact that the Springs were rich enough to gratify their generous impulses was less remarkable than the cheerful simplicity with which they dispensed their treats. Of course Margaret also had some treats for these excellent friends: for instance, she could take the good Marcus to see the great Carlyle, whose works the good man enthusiastically admired.

On August 1, 1846, the party sailed from Boston on the *Cambria*. A voyage on the *Cambria* was in itself an event in those days, and this particular passage was memorable for being the shortest trip yet made across the Atlantic. The time was ten days and sixteen hours from Boston to Liverpool, announced with much celebration and rejoicing by the newspapers.

Margaret and her traveling companions were keen upon the track of reform. They rejoiced in the recent triumph of the Corn Laws and the gathering signs of Chartism in England. Wordsworth was pictured in Margaret's *Tribune* letter as a " reverend old man, clothed in black, and walking with cautious step along the level garden-path " who was not " prepared to say in the matter of the Corn Laws whether existing interests had been as carefully attended to as was just." She went to hear James Martineau preach and described him as one of those " who love the new wine, but do not feel that they can afford to throw away *all* their old bottles." At the Mechanics' Institute in Liverpool, she was enormously pleased to hear *The Dial* quoted by the Director in speaking on the subject of self-culture. She praised the work that the Institute was doing for girls, but she added briefly, "Woman nominally, not really, at the head." From Liverpool also she wrote: "I saw there, too, the body of an infant borne to the grave by women; for it is a beautiful custom here that those who have fulfilled all other tender offices to the little being should hold to it the same relation to the very last."

The London Reform Club was a great adventure to the whole party, especially the marvelous kitchen arrangements, of which Margaret remarked that "Fourier himself might have taken pleasure in them." Mr. Spring was busy taking notes on the steam cooking and washing machinery, which he meant to install in the Red Bank phalanstery on his return home, and which he actually did with great success. Margaret, always peering at symptoms of woman's status, remarks of this wonder-kitchen that there she found women only as the " servants of servants; " but she did not begrudge the chef and his male apprentices their position of supremacy. "I was not sorry, however," she wrote, " to see men predominant in the cooking department, as I hope to see that and washing transferred

to their care in the progress of things, since they are
'the stronger sex'." With Mr. Spring she also
visited model laundries, and they busied themselves
with plans for installing a similar institution in New
York. "One arrangement that they have here in
Paris will be a good one," wrote Margaret, "even
when we cease to have any very poor people, and,
please Heaven, also any very rich. These are the
Crèches,—houses where poor women leave their children to be nursed during the day while they are at
work."

Margaret and her friends, primed with all the ideas
of Fourier, visited the great industries of England and
France and saw for themselves the misery of the
working classes in that terrible year. At Newcastle
they descended into a coal mine and at Sheffield they
went on Saturday night to see the steel-workers paid
off. At Manchester, Margaret went out in the street
at night to talk with the girls from the mills, "who
were strolling bareheaded, with coarse, rude, and
reckless air," and saw "through the windows of the
gin-palaces the women seated drinking, too dull to
carouse." In Lyons, she went into some weavers'
homes, consisting of a single room filled with looms
with the beds on shelves near the ceiling. Of these
women, she said, "There are but two ways open to
them, weaving and prostitution, to gain their bread."

From England, she wrote, " Can any man who has
seen these things dare blame the Associationists for
their attempt to find prevention against such misery
and wickedness in our land," and by the time she had
reached Paris, she was of the opinion that " erelong
help must be sought by other means than words."

Margaret's visit to Harriet Martineau was described
by the latter in one of the most lively passages of
her autobiography. She expressed her opinion of
Margaret's manners and criticized her behavior as a
guest at Ambleside with the warmest animosity. Indeed, her resentment was somewhat excusable owing
to Margaret's unpleasant candor with regard to her
book *Society in America,* published in 1836. The
book had exasperated not only Margaret but many
of the author's American friends; and Margaret with
her customary candor had written Miss Martineau a
frank letter.

" I got the book as soon as it came out," she wrote,
" long before I received the copy endeared by your
handwriting, and devoted myself to reading it. I gave
myself up to my natural impressions, without seeking
to ascertain those of others. . . . Certainly you
show no spirit of harshness towards this country in
general. . . . But many passages are reformed by
intemperance of epithet. . . . Would your heart,
could you but investigate the matter, approve such

overstatement, such a crude, intemperate tirade as you have been guilty of about Mr. Alcott,—a true and noble man, a philanthropist, whom a true and noble woman, also a philanthropist, should have delighted to honor; whose disinterested and resolute efforts, for the redemption of poor humanity, all independent and faithful minds should sustain, since the ' broadcloth' vulgar will be sure to assail them; . . . a man whom the worldlings of Boston hold in as much horror as the worldlings of ancient Athens did Socrates. They smile to hear their verdict confirmed from the other side of the Atlantic, by their censor, Harriet Martineau. . . .

" I have thought it right to say all this to you, since I felt it. I have shrunk from the effort, for I fear that I must lose you. . . . I know it must be so trying to fail of sympathy, at such a time, where we expect it. And, besides, I felt from the book that the sympathy between us is less general than I had supposed, it was so strong on several points. It is strange enough for me to love you ever, and I could no more have been happy in your friendship, if I had not spoken out now."

It is scarcely necessary to say that the friendship which survived this piece of correspondence was cool and formal to a degree. Nevertheless, Miss Martineau pretended to herself that she had forgotten all about the painful episode when Margaret appeared at Ambleside ten years later. " I am sure I met her with every desire for friendly intercourse," Miss Martineau protests. Yet Margaret, it appears, from her hostess's lively reminiscences, behaved atrociously. She and the Springs had lodgings in the village, but Miss Martineau otherwise did the honors as hostess. Margaret's companions, we are told, evidently enjoyed themselves (they had that faculty) but Margaret as evidently did not. One day she would insist on haranguing the whole party incessantly and on the next she would not speak a word to anyone. As Miss Martineau, aided by her convenient deafness, was herself an incessant and uninterruptable talker, her comments on Margaret's loquaciousness have the familiar flavor of the pot who called the kettle black. At the same time, Margaret's manners, always too aggressive to be really ladylike, were doubtless not improved by the emotional crisis in which she found herself at this particular time, owing to the position of her affairs with the errant Mr. Nathan.

The real business in hand between Margaret and her Ambleside hostess was mesmerism. Miss Martineau's experience with the black art and her public defense of it was a notorious Victorian scandal. Margaret's visit to her was in the nature of an assignment. She had to report back to the *Tribune* readers on the state of Miss Martineau's health. The facts of the story are briefly these. After five years of helpless invalidism, which had baffled the doctors, Miss Martineau had been restored to complete health by a short mesmeric treatment under the direction of Mr. Atkinson. As she triumphantly puts it, she had " come back unharmed from the land of dreams, . . . while the medical world was hoping to hear of her insanity." Naturally the medical world resented her inexplicable cure, and the public resented it also. It took a good deal of courage to be on Miss Martineau's side, but Margaret was on her side and so was Elizabeth Barrett. " Carlyle calls Harriet Martineau quite mad because of her belief in mesmerism," wrote Miss Barrett; " for my own part, I am not afraid to say that I almost believe in mesmerism and quite believe in Harriet Martineau." And Margaret sent her report on the historic case to the *Tribune* in these words : " From the testimony of those who were with her in and since her illness, her recovery would seem to be of as magical quickness and sure progress as has been represented." Nevertheless Margaret was somewhat puzzled by the case. She noted in her private journal, " The look of health in her face, but a harried, excited, over-stimulated state of mind."

The truth about Harriet Martineau's illness, of course, was that it was of an hysterical nature, as

Margaret's ill-health was hysterical, and Elizabeth Barrett's, and Thomas Carlyle's, and poor, wasted, brilliant Jane Carlyle's. Harriet Martineau's narrative of how she fell ill is enough to explain the success of her cure, so far as there was a cure. She lived at home with her mother in the rôle of a dutiful daughter until the age of thirty-eight. Her mother, being blind and exigent, was a most trying parent. Harriet, in the meantime, had become a celebrated author and an active influence in public affairs. The strain of her home life became unendurable; "Heaven knows," she exclaims, "I never sought fame, and I would thankfully have given it all away in exchange for domestic peace and ease. But there it was!" Obviously there was no escape from her filial duties but to fall ill, which she did, and with complete thoroughness and success. Broken in health, she was compelled to remain at the seashore separated from her mother, and her condition, in spite of the sea air, made no improvement. She suffered for months from the most terrible dreams, in which she seemed to see her mother fall from a precipice, or a staircase, or a church-steeple, and to feel that it was her fault. She wished to show by these dreams how over-anxious and over-dutiful had been her attendance on her beloved parent, but the modern Freudian recognizes in them the revelation of a secret wish which struggled

for birth into consciousness, and can thereby understand the intensity of the mental conflict to which the
health of the faithful daughter had at last succumbed.
But mesmerism was the nearest approach to the truth
which the year 1846 offered as a clue to illnesses like
these and one must give credit to the intelligence of
those who, like Harriet Martineau and Margaret
Fuller, took it seriously.

Margaret apparently was not mesmerized while at
Ambleside, though it seems incredible that with her
thirst for experience she should have allowed the opportunity to slip. Miss Martineau, who might have
tried her hand on Margaret as she did—with considerable success—on Charlotte Brontë, was not sufficiently *en rapport* with her guest. That is clear. But
the fascinating and philosophical Mr. Atkinson, who
was responsible for Miss Martineau's cure, was also
there and he found in Margaret a most sympathetic
listener. "The professed magnetizer with his *beaux
yeux* and extreme sensibility," she wrote, "unable
to confer benefit without receiving injury, gave me
yet another view of this grand subject." Perhaps
Margaret's keen enthusiasm for "the prince of the
English mesmerizers" as she called him, did not par-
ticularly increase her hostess's good-will towards her
on this occasion. The *rapport* between herself and
Mr. Atkinson continued excellent, as she afterwards

saw a good deal of him in London. Still there is no indication in Margaret's notes that she was mesmerized by Mr. Atkinson. Did Miss Martineau fail to encourage it? For she was also in London, and now quite angry with Margaret, who treated her, she said, like a *commonplace* person. But even without the attainment of the mesmeric *rapport,* Margaret's enthusiastic appreciation of Mr. Atkinson was not without certain happy results for her widowed state of mind. To a confidential friend at home she wrote, " As soon as I reached England, I found how right you were in supposing there was elsewhere a greater range of interesting character among the men, than with us." She added a description of Miss Martineau's mesmerizer, " with a head for Leonardo to paint ", spoke of some artists she had met, and ended by giving the palm to Mazzini. " By far the most beauteous person I have seen is Joseph Mazzini." At the same time she sent a cool message to Mr. James Nathan, her quondam lover, through a common friend, that she had received his letter, " but was too much involved in the routine of visiting and receiving visitors to allow her mind a moment's repose to reply to it."

For years Margaret had been greatly impressed by the peculiar invalidism of two English women. " Another interesting sign of the time," she had written, " is the influence exercised by two women, Miss Martineau and Miss Barrett, from their sick-rooms. The lamp of life which, if it had been fed only by the affections, and depended on precarious human relations, would scarce have been able to maintain a feeble glare in the lonely prison, now shines far and wide over the nations, cheering fellow-sufferers and hallowing the joy of the healthful." This was all very well, but in reaching England she found that both of her celebrated invalids, who had been so independent of their affections and of precarious human relations, had suddenly ceased to be invalids, resumed their human relations, and developed their affections. As soon as she left Miss Martineau, she went at once to Miss Barrett with her letters of introduction only to find that she, as well as Miss Martineau, had made a spectacular recovery. Margaret posted a letter back to Mr. Duyckinck in New York at once. " Miss Barrett has just *eloped* with Browning; she had to elope, Mr. Howe says, from a severe, hard father. The influence of this father seems to have been crushing. I hope she may now be happy and well, perhaps I shall see them—her and Browning—in Italy." The elopement of the forty-year-old daughter had brought to light all the details of the father's morbid conduct, —how he had mounted guard over the sick-room, had refused to permit his daughter to move from her sofa, and had prayed over her presumably incurable illness. Margaret arrived in London just in time for the avalanche of gossip which followed the astounding elopement. These events naturally gave her much food for thought concerning the psychic cause and cure of illness. And when she herself went to a performance of Don Giovanni, after having suffered for several days from a severe neuralgic pain and came away realizing that the opera had cured her, she was moved to set down her opinion of these matters in her *Tribune* letter. " Ah! if physicians only understood the influence of the mind over the body, instead of treating, as they so often do, their patients like machines, and according to precedent."

It would seem as if Margaret had every reason to be impressed by this idea during her visit in England. In the home of the Carlyles,—another goal of her pilgrimage,—it was the same story of inexplicable physical misery over again. Only in this case, there seemed to be no cure or amelioration in sight. Margaret must have seen the emotional strain between the Carlyles at its worst for this was the year when Mrs. Carlyle was ready for desperate remedies, and, but for the restraining influence of Mazzini, might have actually deserted. Mazzini told her to go home and find her solace in communion with her dead parents, which she literally did for another twenty years, until she died and was laid beside her father in the Haddington churchyard. Margaret Fuller visited these sad companions midway of the long, unnatural marriage described on Mrs. Carlyle's tombstone thus: " For forty years she was the true and ever-loving help-mate of her husband ". It was a sham marriage to the end, owing to Carlyle's impotence, and the terrible weight of morbidity, the dyspepsia and neuralgia which pursued them like a plague, was the result of the unhealthy asceticism in which they lived.

To Emerson, the Carlyle ménage was idyllic. He had sent Margaret to them with the warmest letters of introduction. Margaret was also introduced by her book on *Woman,* which Jane Carlyle, along with many other Londoners, had read. " I have been received here with a warmth which surprised me," wrote Margaret to Mr. Duyckinck, " it is chiefly to Woman in the 19th that I am indebted for this." She went to the Carlyles' several times, and recognized that the situation was not idyllic by any means. Of Carlyle, she said, " He seems to me quite isolated, lonely as the desert."

She had never accepted Carlyle at Emerson's valuation. Her review of *Oliver Cromwell* had contained many strictures on Carlyle's views of life and she had read some early letters of his which fell into her hands in Liverpool and which contained, she noted, " very low views of life, comfortable and prudential advice as to marriage, envy of riches, thirst for fame avowed as a leading motive." Now at last she saw him face to face in his home at Chelsea. "For a couple of hours," she said, "he was talking about poetry and the whole harangue was one eloquent proclamation of the defects of his own mind. . . . The most amusing part is when he comes back to some refrain, as in the French Revolution of the *sea-green*. In this instance, it was Petrarch and *Laura,* the last word pronounced with his ineffable sarcasm of drawl. Although he said this over fifty times, I could not help laughing when *Laura* would come,—Carlyle running his chin out, when he spoke it, and his eyes glancing till they looked like the eyes and beak of a bird of prey! Poor Laura! Lucky for her that her poet had already got her safely canonized beyond the reach of this Teufelsdröck vulture." It is a question whether the "Laura" he so bitterly inveighed against was safely out of reach of all this frustrate vindictiveness. "Mrs. Carlyle sat by in silence," Margaret said, "who can speak while her husband is there?"

The Carlyles gave a dinner party in their Chelsea house for Margaret and George Henry Lewes. It was fitting that Mr. Carlyle should thus seek to bring together the two foremost Goethe critics of the day. But the meeting was not a success; certainly there was no *rapport* from Margaret's point of view. Lewes was engaged in writing the Life of Goethe which Margaret had once dreamed of writing but had been forced to abandon for school-teaching in Providence. George Eliot was not at the party; she had not yet come to London, being still at home in Coventry with her aged father. Lewes antagonized Margaret Fuller at first sight, as much as he attracted Marian Evans. Margaret never could endure vivacious men. She described him as "a witty, French, flippant sort of man," and as for his writing a Life of Goethe, she thought that "a task for which he must be as unfit as irreligion and sparkling shallowness can make him." Notwithstanding this priggish denunciation of her fellow-critic, who probably had traits uncomfortably suggestive of her own, Margaret's life and Lewes's developed a certain sympathetic relationship in after years. They were both explained as acting in imitation of Goethe in their unconventional marriages. It is also very probable that George Eliot was more directly influenced by Margaret than by the example of Goethe. The following passage in a letter, written to a friend not long before her departure with Lewes for the continent, seems to prove it. "You know how sad one feels when the great procession has swept by one, and the last notes of its music have died away, leaving one alone with the field and sky. I feel so about life sometimes. It is a help to read such a life as Margaret Fuller's. How inexpressibly touching that passage from her Journal,—' I shall always reign through the intellect, but the life! the life! oh, my God! shall that never be sweet?' I am thankful, as if for myself, that it was sweet at last." Thus Margaret's life, despite its tragical end, helped Marian Evans to have the courage to live her own. Destiny made her in spite of herself, the ally of this "witty, French, flippant sort of man" after all.

Margaret and the Springs arrived in Paris in time to spend Christmas there. Here again she found herself not wholly unknown. Her essay on American Literature had been translated into French and published in *La Revue Indépendente,* and Margaret was asked by the editor of the journal to write for it after her return to the United States. She saw La Mennais and Béranger and heard Chopin play. "I went to call on La Mennais, to whom I had a letter," she writes. "I found him in a little study; his secretary was writing in a larger room through which I passed. With him was a somewhat citizen-looking, but vivacious, elderly man, whom I was at first sorry to see, having wished for half-an-hour's undisturbed visit to the apostle of Democracy. But how quickly were those feelings displaced by joy when he named to me the great national lyrist of France, the unequaled

Béranger. I had not expected to see him at all, for he is not one to be seen in any show place; he lives in the hearts of the people, and needs no homage from their eyes. I was very happy in that little study in the presence of these two men, whose influence has been so great, so real."

One of Margaret's most vivid Parisian adventures was in the dentist's chair. Perhaps because she had failed to try mesmerism in England, she now had to try ether in Paris. "After suffering several days very much with the toothache, I resolved to get rid of the cause of sorrow by the aid of ether; not sorry, either, to try its efficacy, after all the marvelous stories I had heard. The first time I inhaled it, I did not for several seconds feel the effect, and was just thinking, 'Alas! this has not power to soothe nerves so irritable as mine,' when suddenly I wandered off, I don't know where, but it was a sensation like wandering in long garden-walks, and through many alleys of trees,—many impressions, but all pleasant and serene. The moment the tube was removed, I started into consciousness, and put my hand to my cheek; but, sad! the throbbing tooth was still there. The dentist said I had not seemed to him insensible. He then gave me the ether in a stronger dose, and this time, I quitted the body instantly, and cannot remember any detail of what I saw and did; but the impression was as in the Oriental tale, where the man has his head in the water an instant only, but in his vision a thousand years seem to have passed. I experienced that same sense of an immense length of time and succession of impressions. . . . Suddenly I seemed to see the old dentist, as I had for the moment before I inhaled the gas, amid his plants, in his night-cap and dressing-gown; in the twilight the figure had somewhat of a Faust-like, magical air, and he seemed to say, ' C'est inutile.' Again I started up, fancying that once more he had not dared to extract the tooth, but it was gone. What is worth noticing is the mental translation I made of his words, which my ear must have caught, for my companion tells me he said, ' C'est la moment,' a phrase of just as many syllables, but conveying just the opposite sense."

The climax of Margaret's experiences in Paris,—perhaps the real climax of her life,—was her meeting with George Sand. At first Madame Sand was at her château in the country and Margaret despaired of seeing her. " At last, however, she came; and I went to see her at her house, Place d'Orléans. I found it a handsome modern residence. She had not answered my letter, written about a week before, and I felt a little anxious lest she should not receive me; for she is too much the mark of impertinent curiosity, as well as too busy, to be easily accessible to strangers. I am by no means timid, but I have suffered, for the first time in France, some of the torments of *mauvaise honte,* enough to see what they must be to many.

"The servant who admitted me was in the picturesque costume of a peasant, and, as Madame Sand afterward told me, her goddaughter, whom she had brought from her province. She announced me as, 'Madame Salere,' and returned into the anteroom to tell me, 'Madame says she does not know you.' I began to think I was doomed to a rebuff, among the crowd who deserve it. However, to make assurance sure, I said, 'Ask if she has not received a letter from me?'

"As I spoke, Madame Sand opened the door and stood looking at me an instant. Our eyes met. I shall never forget her look at that moment. The doorway made a frame for her figure; she is large, but well-formed. She was dressed in a robe of dark violet silk, with a black mantle on her shoulders, her beautiful hair dressed with the greatest taste, her whole appearance and attitude, in its simple, and ladylike dignity, presenting an almost ludicrous contrast to the vulgar caricature of George Sand. Her face is very little like the portraits, but much finer; the upper part of the forehead and eyes are beautiful, the lower, strong and masculine, expressive of a hardy temperament and strong passions, but not in the least coarse;

the complexion olive, and the air of the whole head
Spanish (as, indeed, she was born at Madrid, and is
only on one side of French blood). All these details
I saw at a glance; but what fixed my attention was
the expression of *goodness,* nobleness, and power, that
pervaded the whole; the truly human heart and nature
that shone in the eyes. As our eyes met, she said,
' C'est vous ', and held out her hand. I took it, and
went into her little study; we sat down a moment,
then I said, ' Il me fait de bien de vous voir ', and I
am sure I said it with my whole heart, for it made
me very happy to see such a woman, so large and so
developed a character, and everything that is good
in it so *really* good. I loved, shall always love
her. . . .

" She was very much pressed for time, as she was
then preparing copy for the printer; and, having just
returned, there were many applications to see her, but
she wanted me to stay then, saying, ' It is better to
throw things aside and seize the present moment '. I
stayed a good part of the day, and was very glad
afterwards, for I did not see her again uninter-
rupted. . . .

" Her daughter is just about to be married. It is
said, there is no congeniality between her and her
mother; but for her son she seems to have much love,
and he loves and admires her extremely. . . .

" I heartily enjoyed the sense of so rich, so prolific, so ardent a genius. I liked the woman in her, too, very much.; I never liked a woman better. For the rest, I do not care to write about it much, for I cannot, in the room and time I have to spend, express my thoughts as I would; but as near as I can express the sum-total, it is this. S—— and others who admire her, are anxious to make a fancy picture of her, and represent her as a Helena (in the Seven Chords of the Lyre); all whose mistakes are the fault of the present state of society. But to me, the truth seems to be this. She has that purity in her soul, for she knows well how to love and prize its beauty; but she herself is quite another sort of person. She needs no defense, but only to be understood, for she has bravely acted out her nature, and always with good intentions. She might have loved one man permanently, if she could have found one contemporary with her who could interest and command her throughout her range; but there was hardly a possibility for that, for such a person. Thus she has naturally changed the objects of her affection, and several times. Also there may have been something of the Bacchante in her life, and of the love of night and storm, and the free raptures amid which roamed on the mountain-tops the followers of Cybele, the great goddess, the great mother. But she was never coarse, never gross, and I am sure her generous heart has not failed to draw some rich drops from every kind of wine-press. When she has done with an intimacy, she likes to break it off suddenly, and this has happened often, both with men and women. Many calumnies upon her are traceable to this cause.

"I forgot to mention that, while talking, she *does* smoke all the time her little cigarette. This is now a common practice among ladies abroad, but I believe originated with her.

"For the rest, she holds her place in the literary and social world of France like a man, and seems full of energy and courage in it. I suppose she has suffered much but she has also enjoyed and done much, and her expression is one of calmness and happiness."

Margaret had of course had many varying accounts of George Sand before she saw her face to face. In London she had had the view of Mazzini who was George Sand's great advocate and defender before the British public and to whom Sand seemed the "voice of down-trodden womanhood." Margaret's vision was as little confused by the martyr's halo as by the caricatures; she saw the woman as she was.

CHAPTER IX

HER DEBT TO NATURE

On the journey from Paris to Italy, Margaret made two stops. The first was in Lyons, where she visited the weavers' garrets and saw with her own eyes what she had heard of in Paris. The second stop was at Avignon, where, finding "the banks of the Rhone still sheeted with white," she "waded through melting snow to Laura's tomb."

At last, she was in Italy, at Arles. "I saw the little saxifrage blossoming on the steps of the amphitheater, and fruit trees in flower amid the tombs. Here for the first time I saw the great handwriting of the Romans and its proper medium of stone, and I was content. It looked as grand and solid as I expected, as if life in those days was worth the having, the enjoying, and the using."

Margaret Fuller must be included in the long list of famous people who have loved Italy and Rome with all the ardor of a personal love. This list includes Hannibal and Winkelmann, Shelley and Byron, Elizabeth Barrett and Margaret Fuller, Goethe and Freud. "I may say that only in Rome have I felt what it is to be a man," said Goethe in his old age. "Compared with my situation at Rome I may say I have never since known happiness." As a school-mistress at Providence, Margaret had translated these words and they had got into her blood, intensifying a longing early derived from her childhood acquaintance with the classics. All the romanticists of Margaret's generation made love to Rome. "Rome, my Rome, city of the soul," said Byron; and amid the austerities of New England life, Margaret's homesickness for Rome developed an actual intention. Rome, the glamorous, the unattainable—all imaginative souls who chafed under the repressions of a Puritan civilization dreamed of Rome as the symbol of love and freedom. The motivation of all this passion for a place is analyzed by Freud, out of his own experience, for apparently he has himself known the pains and pleasures of this peculiar Rome-wish. He tells how he used to dream of going to Rome, and adds, "I suppose I shall still have to satisfy this longing by means of dreams for a long time to come." Some years afterwards, he added this illuminating footnote: "I have long since learned that it only requires a little courage to fulfil even such unattainable wishes." This passage from Freud expresses Margaret's feelings, when, after all the long years of delay she at last found herself in the promised land.

But emotional ideals, however firmly rooted in the instincts, cannot stand up empty any more than meal-sacks. Margaret brought to Italy and the Italian situation an educational equipment of which an Italian citizen might well have been proud. She was well-read in Dante, Petrarch, Tasso, Foscolo, Alfieri, Manzoni, and Mazzini. Italy was crowded with memories for her; she had been there so often through the medium of books and the lives of her heroes. "We climbed the hill to Assisi," she writes. "I looked back and saw the carriage toiling up the steep path, drawn by a pair of those light-colored oxen Shelley so much admired. I stood near the spot where Goethe met with a little adventure, which he has described with even more than his usual delicate humor. Who can ever be alone for a moment in Italy?" All her life had been a preparation for this visit. At last, on her thirty-seventh birthday, her goal was achieved and she found herself in Rome.

During the month of May, she grew familiar with every aspect of St. Peter's,—the view from the dome over the city and "its Campagna, its villas with their cypresses and pines serenely sad as is nothing else in the world." She loved the torch-lit scene of the "stone popes where they lie on their tombs, and the old mosaics, and virgins with gilt caps" . . . "St. Peter's," she said, "is a mixture of sublimest heaven with corruptest earth;" the hours she spent there were "the splendidest part of her life."

In this mood, she encountered a very handsome stranger after vespers on Holy Thursday and walked home with him from the Vatican to the Corso. Mrs. Story wrote a careful account of how Margaret was looking for her friends, the Springs, peering through her glasses at the crowd, when a gallant young Italian came up and offered his services. But the Springs had conveniently disappeared, there was no carriage in the usual place outside, and so the chivalrous stranger escorted the American lady to her lodgings. The next day he was seen walking past the house, after which the affair lost its clandestine air and the young man became conventionally attached to the party as Margaret's constant caller and attentive escort.

He turned out to be an impoverished Marchese, about ten years younger than Margaret, and the youngest son of the family. He had three older brothers, who were in the Papal service, while the old Marquese was the official head of a Roman *rione* or ward. Thus it appears that the Ossolis were considerably involved in Roman politics, which must have had a familiar appeal for Margaret. Old Ossoli was in his last illness when she appeared on the scene, and Angelo, still living at home without any definite career, was engaged in nursing his father. The old

Marquese died, and Margaret received the young man straight from the hands of his father, as he was, without ability or ambition in any direction, with intense and clinging affections, and with unusual personal beauty. An American sculptor in Rome declared that Ossoli was the most beautiful man he had ever seen.

He was absolutely without vivacity, being reserved and silent in his manners and marked by a rather melancholy expression. Though Margaret often reproached Emerson because he would not laugh " in a cordial human fashion," she never really liked any man who did. Her young Roman, whom she had traveled so far to find, was as much of a Puritan in manners and disposition as if she had found him in Cambridgeport. Writing to her mother, Margaret said that Ossoli had ways that reminded her of her brother Eugene.

To a bluestocking like Margaret, who had sacrificed the very best years of her life to putting her brothers through college and who inherited a supreme reverence for the Harvard degree, the ignorance of her Ossoli must have seemed appalling. His education had been in the hands of a lazy priest who had neglected him, so that books and reading played no part in his grown-up life. By the side of the woman who read " at a rate like Gibbon's," her handsome

lover seemed almost illiterate; but by the side of the
average gentleman of his own class in Italy, perhaps
his education would have made a much better showing. One cannot know; one only knows that Margaret, anxious not to over-praise him in her letters
home, for obvious reasons, explained that he had no
intellectual interests and no taste for books. Antici-
pating the first impression he would make on her
Transcendental friends, she may have even under-
estimated his abilities in the hope of creating a favorable rather than a disappointing surprise.

The facts, however, are that Ossoli played the part
of a judicious conspirator and a brave officer in the
Roman Revolution. But, though he joined the liberals in fighting the Pope, he clung to his ancestral
religion and cherished its fantasies and superstitions.
He went regularly to vesper service, even after his
marriage, and Margaret, far from discouraging his
simple piety, often went with him. She respected
what she described as the "profound myths" of the
Catholic Church. "Indeed," she remarked, "such
things need to be judged of by another standard than
the Connecticut Blue-Laws". Margaret herself had
traveled a long way from the Puritanical standards of
her early environment. She could comprehend George
Sand and the Roman Catholic Church, and knew that
humanity included more things than the code of John

Cotton had ever dreamed of. Henry James said, "There might be ways for her of being vivid that were not as the ways of Boston."

After the meeting with Ossoli in May, Margaret and her friends left Rome in June, journeying northward. The plan was to visit Assisi, Perugia, Florence, Bologna, Venice, Verona, Mantua, and Milan; after that, Switzerland; then Germany; and from there back to England before returning home. But no sooner had the party arrived in Florence than Margaret began to lay plans for returning to Rome. At first, she decided to go with her companions as far as Switzerland and then turn back for the autumn. But she ended by falling ill in Venice, and stopping there while the Springs went on according to their original plans. She followed along the same route later, stopping long enough in Milan to become deeply interested in revolutionary plans in which Milan was already far advanced. She spent the summer's end in Switzerland, and by the first of October was back in Rome and settled for the winter in a furnished room, which she dignified by the name of an "apartment."

With her decision to desert the Springs, she gave up all the comforts and conveniences of traveling in their company. She wrote to her brother for four hundred dollars and planned to make it last her six months. "I should always suffer the pain of Tantalus, thinking of Rome, if I could not see it more thoroughly than I have as yet even begun to." She took a room again in the Corso, where she could see all the motions of Rome " in tranquil companionship, not in the restless impertinence of sight-seeing." In the same strain, she wrote to Marcus Spring in Germany, which had lost all charm for Margaret. " All other places faded away, now that I again saw St. Peter's and heard the music of the fountains." She found some encouragement for her recklessness in a meeting with William Wetmore Story, also late of Boston, who had finally given up the law for an artist's life in Italy.

Margaret's intimacy with Angelo Ossoli dated from her return to Rome. Apparently she did not intend to be married to him, for she regarded the marriage as unsuitable in many ways. The difference in their ages and interests and the similarity in their poverty made the union seem impossible. But her fate pursued her swiftly and before Christmas, she knew that she was to have a child. What she had entered upon as a perishable romance would have to be perpetuated as life-long common struggle for existence. Her four hundred dollars for six months was suddenly most pitifully inadequate ; Ossoli, it seems, had no resources ; and the kind, affectionate Springs were too far away to help. In her crisis, she could look nowhere for protection and aid. She wrote to her old friend Caroline Sturgis all but the actual facts of her situation. " I have known some happy hours, but they all lead to sorrow; and not only the cups of wine, but of milk, seem drugged with poison for me. It does not *seem* to be my fault, this Destiny; I do not court these things,—they come. I am a poor magnet, with power to be wounded by the bodies I attract. . . .

" When I arrived in Rome, I was at first intoxicated to be here. The weather was beautiful, and many circumstances combined to place me in a kind of passive, childlike well-being. That is all over now, and, with this year, I enter upon a sphere of my destiny so difficult, that I, at present, see no way out, except through the gate of death. It is useless to write of it; you are at a distance and cannot help me;—whether accident or angel will, I have no intimation. I have no reason to hope I shall not reap what I have sown, and do not. Yet how I shall endure it I cannot guess; it is all a dark, sad enigma. The beautiful forms of art charm no more, and a love, in which there is all fondness but no help, flatters in vain."

The tone of her *Tribune* correspondence showed the depression of her spirits. She described the Christmas festivities and the worship of the Catholic *bambino* with touches of realistic irony. " A faint and misty gleam of sun greeted the day on which there was the feast of the Bambino, the most venerated date of Rome. . . . It has received more splendid gifts than any other idol. An orphan, by my side, now struggling with difficulties [probably the penniless Ossoli] showed me on its breast a splendid jewel, which a doting grandmother thought more likely to benefit her soul if given to the Bambino, than if turned into money to give her grandchildren education and prospects in life." She went again to the grand feast in honor of the Bambino and watched with a peculiar fascination a man who knelt long with bowed head before the image and seemed to her to be in an anguish of prayer, as she said, " either from repentance or anxiety." " I wished I could have hoped the ugly little doll would do him any good," she added, rather spitefully.

Her attentions to the rich Bambino during Christmas week were varied by a visit to another church to see a nun take the veil. " The nun, an elegantly dressed woman of five or six and twenty,—pretty enough, but whose quite worldly air gave the idea that it was one of those arrangements made because no suitable establishment could otherwise be given her, —came forward, knelt, and prayed. Her confessor, in that strained, unnatural whine too common among all preachers and all countries, praised himself for having induced her to enter on a path which would lead her fettered steps from palm to palm, from triumph to triumph! Poor thing! She looked as if domestic olives and poppies were all she wanted, and lacking these, tares and wormwood must be her portion. She was then taken behind a grating, her hair cut, and her clothes exchanged for the nun's vestments; the black-robed sisters who worked upon her looking like crows or ravens at their ominous feast. . . . The effect on my mind was revolting and painful to the last degree." She dwelt at length on the horror of this young woman's future, in order to reassure herself, no doubt, and ended with the statement that it was her own conviction,—that "the snares of the world are less dangerous than the demons of solitude." Margaret had tried both in her life, and she realized that her present situation with its actual dangers was safer after all than her solitary year of fantasies in Boston, with its midnight visitants from other worlds and its mystic ecstasies. With her characteristic honesty, she wrote to Emerson, "Some years ago, I thought you were unjust, because you did not lend faith to my spiritual experiences; but I see you were quite right."

But her consciousness of fulfilment was her only solace in the midst of difficulties. The romantic glamour had fled from her world; the picturesque drama of Catholicism had lost its savor. It was a real comfort now to criticize the show. The Church, for all its Madonna worship and its veneration of female saints, did not provide proper seats for women, she said. " All the good seats were for the men in the area below, but in the gallery windows and from the organ loft, a few women were allowed to peep at what was going on. I was one of these exceptional characters." She forgot all about her recent criticisms of those objectionable Americans who could not appreciate the poetry and symbolism of the Church and joined their company. " There was once a soul in the religion while the blood of its martyrs was yet fresh on the ground, but that soul was always too much encumbered with the remains of pagan habits and customs; that soul is now quite fled elsewhere and in the splendid catafalco, watched by so many white and red-robed snuff-taking, sly-eyed men, would they let it be opened, nothing would be found but bones!"

Her marriage with Ossoli took place at some date which Margaret never revealed. Her friend, Mrs. Story, afterwards said it had occurred in December, but this could not have been correct, as Margaret would have had no reason in that case for concealing it. This is all the more remarkable, as she must have known in December that the marriage was necessary. Her reluctance to confirm the tie by marriage must have been exceedingly great, that she should thus have complicated matters by further postponement.

It was true that a legalized union, openly acknowledged, involved a pecuniary risk for them. The Ossoli estate had not yet been settled and Margaret's husband would certainly have been cut off from his portion for having married a Protestant and a radical. Afterwards Margaret gave this as her reason for having so long concealed the marriage. " But," she wrote to her Italian friend, Madame Arconati, *" to you,* I add, this is only half the truth." She waited until her child was a year old before she made her announcement, and then withheld the date.

There is not the least hint that the gentlemanly Ossoli shirked the situation in any regard. On the contrary, his fidelity and affection were unswerving. Without doubt Ossoli was in love. Margaret did not find herself at any time in the conventional rôle of Gretchen; her husband was her ally against society. Whatever the unknown details were, the affair did not turn out as moralists would predict. There is a common assumption that a young man cannot entertain a romantic attachment for an older woman. So strongly established is this opinion that we find Margaret's biographers preoccupied with proofs that Ossoli really *did* love his American wife and that he did not marry her for her money! Even the testimony of the American consul at Turin is solemnly brought forward. He wrote to Mr. Emerson, who apparently wanted to be shown, " It is abundantly evident that her young husband discharged all the obligations of his relation to her *con amore*. His admiration amounted to veneration, and her yearning to be loved seemed at last to be satisfied." Whether the consular seal helped to convince Emerson is unfortunately not on record.

The puzzle was a double one. It had two members: How could Ossoli marry a woman so much older than himself and altogether without beauty? and, How could Margaret, with all her culture, marry a man without intellect or education? The answer to the puzzle is that he loved her for her age and dignity and authority, she loved him for his youth and beauty. He filled up the place left vacant in her life by her favorite brother Eugene and she restored in his the long-cherished maternal image. Margaret wrote to her mother this description of her husband: " He has, I think, even a more holy feeling about a mother, from having lost his own, when very small. It has been a life-long want with him. He often shows me a little scar on his face, made by a jealous dog, when his mother was caressing him as an infant. He prizes that blemish much." On the basis of these older and more intense relationships, they had discovered a pro-

ple coming in to see me because they don't know what to do with themselves. I am very glad to see them for the same reason; this atmosphere is so heavy, I seem to carry the weight of the world on my head and feel unfitted for every exertion. As to eating, that is a by-gone thing; wine, coffee, meat, I have resigned; vegetables are few and hard to have, except horrible cabbage, in which the Romans delight. A little rice still remains, which I take with pleasure, remembering it growing in the rich fields of Lombardy, so green and full of glorious light. That light fell still more beautiful on the tall plantations of hemp, but it is dangerous just at present to think of what is made from hemp."

By May her health and spirits were restored and she was able to work at her writing-table again, setting down her current impressions. " I sit in my obscure corner, and watch the progress of events. . . . Everything confirms me in my radicalism; and, without any desire to hasten matters, indeed with surprise to see them rush so like a torrent I seem to see them tending to realize my own hopes! . . . It would appear that the political is being merged in the social struggle: it is well."

Early in the summer, Margaret left Rome and went up into the Abruzzi mountains. She settled in Aquila, planning to await there the birth of her child and to work on her book. June in Aquila was radiantly beautiful. " I am in the midst of a theater of glorious snow-crowned mountains, whose pedestals are garlanded with the olive and mulberry, and along whose sides run bridle-paths, fringed with almond groves and vineyards. The valleys are yellow with saffron flowers; the grain fields enameled with the brilliant blue corn-flower and red poppy. . . . The spirits of the dead crowd me in most solitary places." Most of her time was devoted to writing, but several hours of each day were spent out of doors, in walks or in riding on a donkey. She amused herself by telling the peasants the legends of their own saints and the peasants were disturbed about her. " E sempre sola soletta," they said, " eh perche? "

She made the acquaintance of an old nobleman who showed her in his family archives some manuscript letters of Tasso. But as the summer advanced she grew very lonely. " If it were only possible to be nearer to you," she wrote to Ossoli, " for, except for the good air and the security, this place does not please me." In July she moved down into the foot-hills, and settled herself in the village of Rieti, which could be reached by diligence from Rome in one night's journey.

In Rieti, her hard times set in. At first, she saw only the picturesque side of her retreat, " a little, red-brown nest," settled by the aborigines of Italy, "long before Rome was." . . . "The rapid Velino makes almost the circuit of its walls, on its way to Terni. I had my apartment shut out from the family, on the bank of this river, and saw the mountains, as I lay on my restless couch.   There was a piazza, too, or, as they call it here, a loggia, which hung over the river, where I walked most of the night, for I could not sleep at all in those nights.   In the wild autumn storms, the stream became a roaring torrent, constantly lit up by lightning flashes, and the sound of its rush was very sublime.   I see it yet as it swept away on its dark green current the heaps of burning straw which the children let down from the bridge."   Over this bridge came the diligence from Rome, bringing letters and journals from Ossoli and sometimes, on Sunday mornings, the dark young captain himself. "Do not fail to come," says one of Margaret's letters, "I shall have your coffee warm.   You will arrive early, and I can see the diligence pass the bridge from my window."

But Rieti was a village and in some respects not unlike Cambridgeport, as Margaret discovered to her cost.   "At the barber's, the druggist's, the café, they sit and digest the copious slander, chief product of this, as of every *little* hive of men," she said.   Doubtless they suspected some irregularity in the relations between the English lady,—as they took her to be,—and her handsome Roman husband. They also thought that all *Inglesi* were exceedingly rich and plundered poor Margaret in every way. These impressions and suspicions prepared the way for serious consequences when Margaret later left her baby there and was cut off from all communication during the siege of Rome.

From the early part of August, the child was expected. And now a sudden turn in political events threatened to deprive Margaret of her only friend. Pio Nono ordered the civic guard, in which Ossoli was now captain, to go to the defense of Bologna. " My state is the most deplorable that can be," wrote the young man. " I have had an extraordinary struggle. If your condition were not such as it is, I could decide more easily, but in the present moment, I cannot leave you." To which Margaret replied, " If it is possible for you to wait for two or three weeks, the public state will be determined,—as well also mine,—and you can make your decision with more tranquillity. . . . It troubles me much that I can tell you nothing certain of myself, but am still in the same waiting state. . . . If you do not come, I shall expect a letter from you on Sunday, . . . also the last of those Milanese papers. Poor friends, shut up there. I wish so much for some certain intelligence of their fate. . . . Adieu, dear; our misfortunes are many and unlooked for, not often does destiny demand a greater price for some happy moments. Never do I repent of our affection, and for you, if not for me, I hope that life has still some good in store."

The Pope rescinded the order to the troops, and Margaret, in her great relief, found herself a little better. But she could not take much satisfaction in the fact. "It troubles me that this seems rather an indication that I must wait yet longer," she wrote. "*Wait!* That is always hard. But—if I were sure of doing well—I should wish much to pass through this trial before your arrival; yet when I think that it is possible for me to die alone, without the touch of one dear hand, I wish to wait yet longer."

The child was born on Tuesday, September 5, 1848. He was baptized with the name of Angelo Eugene Philip, for his father, his mother's brother Eugene, and the late Marquese, his grandfather. On Thursday, the mother was tormented by his crying; on Saturday, she began to take pleasure in watching him; at the end of twelve days, she was tracing resemblances to his father and herself. At the end of three weeks, she was quite in love with him. The thought of leaving him with strangers became most painful. "He is always so charming, how can I ever, ever leave him? I wake in the night, I look at him, I think, oh! it is impossible to leave him." She was pleased that the child was a boy, though she could not justify her partiality. " As was Eve, at first, I suppose every mother is delighted by the birth of a man-child. There is a hope that he will conquer more ill and effect more good, than is expected from girls. This prejudice in favor of man does not seem to be destroyed by his shortcomings for ages." In the solitude and loneliness of Rieti, the tendency was for her to center all her affection and attention upon the child; so that, after an absence from him, she had to admit that the removal of her maternal solicitude had not been altogether bad for him. " I see that he is more serene, is less sensitive, than with me, and sleeps better," she said, on her return after a separation.

Early in November, when the mountains and ravines were covered with snow, Margaret returned to Rome. The baby was left with his wet-nurse who put him into little black caps and made him into a real peasant *bambino*. Margaret's journey proved a dangerous one, for the Tiber had overflowed its banks and the approaches to Rome were swimming in water. Meadows and roads shone like a sheet of silver in the moonlight. Swimming and plunging, the horses reached the gate at last and the diligence was stopped by the customs officers. Margaret alighted and walked to the Villa Ludovisi and stood looking at the dark myrtle shrubberies and the pale statues under the Roman moon. Her principal emotion was surprise at finding herself again alive and well in the city she so much loved. " Is it not cruel that I cannot earn six hundred dollars a year living here? " was her passionate thought.

She took a room at No. 60, Piazza Barberini, the " quiet, little upper chamber " in which Mrs. Story tells of finding her in March, 1849. Here Margaret spent the winter working on her history of contemporary events and sending long and detailed accounts to the columns of the *Tribune*. Her circumstances seemed unchanged, though it was apparent to the Storys that she lived in the most extreme poverty. The faithful Ossoli was as usual in attendance and the Storys were aware that the two were on an intimate footing. For Margaret wrote to William Story in November soon after her return to Rome, " I have . . . passed this past month of fine weather most delightfully in revisiting my haunts of the autumn before. Then, too, I was uncommonly well and strong; it was the golden period of my Roman life. . . . To you I may tell, that I always go with Ossoli, the most congenial companion I ever had for jaunts of this kind. We go out in the morning, carrying the roast chestnuts from Rome; the bread and wine are found in some lonely little osteria; and so we dine; and reach Rome again, just in time to see it, from a little distance, gilded by the sunset."

But it was not until summer, during the terrible month of the siege, that Margaret told Mrs. Story about her marriage and the child's existence.

In the summer, communication with Rieti became irregular and was finally broken off. "I often seemed to hear Angelino calling to me amid the roar of the cannon and always his tone was of crying," writes Margaret. Day after day, she stood in the long queue at the post-office under the burning sun, but no news came. Her remittances to Rieti had stopped; there was no longer any way of sending money, even if she had had any, which is doubtful. The ignorant foster-mother at Rieti, not unnaturally disposed to suspect the motives of Nino's mysterious parents, became alarmed and wrote a letter to Margaret in which she threatened to abandon the child altogether if money was not sent immediately. The money, wherever it came from, was instantly dispatched; perhaps it was the Storys who came to the rescue. Margaret afterwards declared that all her work during the months of separation from her child had been valueless. "Of at least two volumes written at that time, no line seems of any worth . . . the position of a mother separated from her only child is too frightfully un-natural." And yet at the end of this harrowing experience, when the siege was over and the republic in ruins, Margaret waited to send Mazzini out of the city into safety before she went to the rescue of her little Nino. A mother is after all a complex human being.

At one time, fearing that both Ossoli and herself might succumb to the bombardment, Margaret begged the Storys to take care of Angelino. The certificate which she showed to Mrs. Story on this occasion and which Mrs. Story afterwards described is impossible to explain. It was written in Latin on parchment and signed by a priest; and it stated that Angelo Eugene Ossoli was the legal heir of whatever title and fortune should come to his father. This was the paper which Mr. Higginson referred to as a marriage certificate, thereby provoking from McPhail the sardonic comment that "the name of the heir is not usually specified in such writings." The impressive-looking document, which Margaret herself may have helped to compose and which was signed by the priest who had married them, was a pathetic and ineffectual attempt on her part to outwit what she referred to as the "social inquisition of the United States." A good strong lie would have served her better but it was not in her nature. Because her conscience was so clear, she could not feel the necessity for denying her actions.

When the news of Margaret's marriage reached America in the fall of 1849, Fredrika Bremer was staying with the Springs in New York. Not having known Margaret personally, she was present at the social inquisition in the rôle, more or less, of an outsider. In her letters to her sister she gives us glimpses of what occurred. "A report has reached this country that she [Margaret Fuller] has connected herself with a young man,—she herself is no longer young, being upward of forty,—and a Fourierist or socialist marriage, without the external ceremony, is spoken of; certain it is that the marriage remained secret, and that she has a child, a boy. . . . All this has furnished subject for much conversation among her friends and her enemies."

At first Fredrika was inclined to side with those who suspected the worst—whatever the worst might be. "Margaret Fuller," she informed her sister, "has in her writings asserted the right of woman to her own free development, and to liberty in many cases where, although conformable to the strictest moral code, it would yet be offensive to many in this so-called free country." But later on, she professed to be entirely convinced that Margaret's marriage was quite regular and conventional and enthusiastically told her sister that later news had vindicated the loyal trust of Margaret's old friends. As one reads

Fredrika's second letter, one can imagine the kind and affectionate Springs had been at work behind the scenes. They also sent Margaret a check as a present for her little boy.

But there still remained one question which puzzled Fredrika. She had heard the pros and cons in the social inquisition and now she was allowed to read Margaret's letters to Rebecca Spring, in which the champion of woman's rights described her experiences with love and maternity. "She had been described to me as not sufficiently feminine," says Fredrika, puzzled. "She seems to me almost too much so, too much concentered in that one phase of her being."

The one question which, it appears, neither Fredrika nor the inquisition propounded to themselves was this: after all, what *is* feminine?

CHAPTER X

THE REVOLUTIONIST

As Margaret repeatedly declared, her heart and her ambition were not in her writing. They were in politics. She was an excellent conspirator, combining, as she did, a perfectly sincere and truthful nature with the utmost self-control in the keeping of secrets. Emerson referred to this quality of hers in the letter of introduction which he sent to Carlyle. " I need not, and yet perhaps I need say, that M. F. is the safest of all possible persons who ever took pen in hand; Prince Metternich's closet not closer nor half so honorable." This recommendation had less interest perhaps for the Carlyles than it had for Mazzini whom she met at their house. The Chief had great need of safe and reliable friends in those days, when he controlled a whispering gallery which ran from London to Italy and could outstrip the government itself in the speed of its messages.

Mazzini trusted women especially. He said that he inherited his " republican instincts " from his mother, and in his long life of exile and loneliness, women were among his closest friends and counsellors.

Jane Carlyle, George Sand, Giulia Modena, and Margaret Fuller were among his conspicuous and influential friends. He preached feminism to the Italian workingmen, who needed it sadly enough, in all truth, in these words: " Love and respect woman. Look to her not only for comfort, but for strength and inspiration and the redoubling of your intellectual and moral powers. Blot out from your mind any idea of superiority; you have none. There is no inequality between man and woman; but as often is the case between two men, only different tendencies and special vocations. Woman and man are two notes without which the human chord cannot be struck."

And in England, he preached George Sand to the prudish public opinion—which again was sadly in need of his peculiar mission. " Thanks be to God," he said, " George Sand is a *woman*. . . . In the question . . . of the emancipation of woman, of the determination of her duties and her rights in the world, the materials for decision were wanting to us. . . . All that she feels, all that she dreams, all that she pursues; what sanctifies her or makes her free, what weighs upon her and transforms her true nature, in the present arrangement of society, a woman only could tell us. . . . Madame Sand is the first who has boldly entered the arena. . . . As a woman, she has declared to us the secret of her sex, its inward life in all its phases, under all circumstances, and she has thus prepared the way to a just conception of the special mission reserved to her sex—of the duties and special rights which have fallen to its share."

A man who could write like this could not fail to win Margaret's allegiance. From the first moment of meeting him in London, she was absolutely devoted. In a certain sense, she was more strongly attached to Mazzini than she was to Ossoli, and if she had had to choose between them, Ossoli would certainly have been left in peace with his conservative family. Margaret was with the Chief against the world. One evening in London Mazzini was with her when Carlyle, having just returned from a visit to Lord Ashburton's, also called. Margaret sat by silently while Carlyle belabored Mazzini's idealism with scorn and invective. Jane Carlyle was also present, and also silent. "We all felt distant from him," says Margaret, naïvely including Carlyle's wife. At last Mrs. Carlyle turned to Margaret and said, "These are but opinions to Carlyle; but to Mazzini, who has given his all, and helped bring his friends to the scaffold in pursuit of such subjects, it is a matter of life and death."

While the revolution in Rome was at its height and Mazzini was hard pressed by enemies and weighted by discouragements, Margaret one day sent him a letter which has been often quoted by Mazzini's biographers as typical of the warm loyalty he inspired in women. "What emboldens me," she wrote, "is the persuasion that the best friends, in point of sympathy and intelligence,—the only friends of a man of ideas and of marked character,—must be women. You have your mother, no doubt you have others, perhaps many. Of that, I know nothing; only I like to offer also my tribute of affection. When I think that only two years ago you thought of coming into Italy with us in disguise, it seems very glorious that you are about to enter republican Rome as a Roman citizen. . . .

"Dear Mazzini,—you do not return to sleep under the sod of Italy, but to see your thoughts springing up all over the soil. . . . You speak of 'few and late years', but some full ones still remain. A century is not needed, nor should the same man, in the same form of thought, work too long on an age. He would mold and bind it too much to himself. . . . Men like you, appointed ministers, must not be less earnest in their work. Yet to the greatest, the day, the moment is all their kingdom. God takes care of the increase. Farewell! For your sake I could wish at this moment to be an Italian and a man of action."

It has been said that Mazzini's political ideas were all contained in the writings of Dante. If this be true, his leading ideas had been familiar to Margaret from her earliest youth. He was to her the new incarnation of the republican tradition which had been worshiped by father and daughter in the Groton farmhouse. The defender of Brutus and the lover of Beethoven had naturally developed into the disciple of Mazzini. The ideals which blazed forth in the fiery pamphlets of " Young Italy " she had long ago learned to reverence in Cambridgeport, when Timothy Fuller fared forth to air them in Fourth of July orations.

Rome was a part of Mazzini's religion. " Rome has always been a sort of talisman for me," he said. He believed that it was the mission of Rome to lead in the social regeneration of Europe. " After the Rome of the Emperors, after the Rome of the Popes, will come the Rome of the People." The people, he believed, must form the universal family; and only after the republicanization and unification of Europe would true social equality be possible. He had the passionate patriotism of the exile, desiring intensely that Italy should become the first republic of Europe. For the realization of these ideals, he gave up the quiet literary vocation which appealed so strongly to him and assumed the toils and burdens of a political agitator and revolutionary leader. Considering Mazzini's position in history, it is rather surprising to find Emerson writing to Margaret at the climax of

Mazzini's career in Rome and asking her if she did not wish that Italy had a great man. Emerson evidently took Mazzini at Carlyle's valuation. Margaret replied without hesitation, " Mazzini is a great man. In mind, a great poetic statesman; in heart, a lover; in action, decisive and full of resource as Cæsar."

Early in March of 1849, Mazzini came to Rome and went at once to visit Margaret in her quiet little upper chamber in the Piazza Barberini. Ossoli was present, and Mazzini confided to them thus early his fears for the ultimate success of the revolution. The next day, Margaret wrote to Marcus Spring, " Last night Mazzini came to see me. You will have heard how he was called to Italy, and received at Leghorn like a prince, as he is. It is expected that, if the republic lasts, he will be President. . . .

" The labels bearing, in giant letters, *Giuseppe Mazzini, cittadino Romano,* are yet up all over Rome. . . . Last night I heard a ring; then somebody speak my name; the voice struck upon me at once. . . . He stayed two hours, and we talked, though rapidly, of everything. . . . If anyone can save Italy from her foes, inward and outward, it will be he. But he is very doubtful whether this is possible; the foes are too many, too strong, too subtle." This was Margaret's account of the visit. Presumably she told him about her personal affairs and the child at Rieti on this occasion, for she had friends within the revolutionary party who knew about her situation all the time. Naturally she would have told her story to the amiable Italian, as he was known to have the gift of receiving confidences from his women friends.

It was worthy of Margaret's critical intelligence that she could see the shortcomings of her idol and frankly define his limitations. She herself never lost sight of the economic aspect of public events. In her study of the position of her sex, she had emphasized the effect of economic, much more than the effect of political, subjection, and, to her mind, Mazzini did not sufficiently concern himself with economic factors. While Mazzini lingered with the spirit of English liberalism, Margaret's mind was sweeping forward with the current of French socialism. One finds her writing to the *Tribune* like this: "Mazzini has a mind far in advance of his times in general, and his nation in particular. . . . And yet Mazzini sees not all; he aims at political emancipation; but he sees not, perhaps would deny, the bearing of some events, which even now begin to work their way. Of this, more anon; but not today, nor in the small print of the *Tribune*. Suffice it to say, I allude to that of which the cry of Communism, the system of Fourier, and so forth are but forerunners." Margaret foresaw that

This was Margaret's official position throughout
the siege. She spent eight hours daily in the wards
and frequently added night duty as well. Her self-
sacrificing devotion to the wounded and their grateful
appreciation of her services has been dwelt upon at
length by her biographers. It was a part of her
peculiar gift to inspire young men with courage. But
nursing was not after all her especial contribution.
Her opportunity was the revolution itself and her task
was its vindication.

But, while she pleaded for Mazzini's ideals in her
New York newspaper, her soul was privately appalled
at the terrible human cost. She wrote to William
Henry Channing, "You say, you are glad I have had
this great opportunity for carrying out my principles.
Would it were so! I found myself inferior in fortitude and courage to the occasion. I know not how
to bear the havoc and anguish incident to the struggle
for these principles. I rejoiced that it lay not with
me to cut down the trees, to destroy the Elysian gardens, for the defense of Rome; I do not know that I
could have done it. And the sight of those far nobler
growths, the beautiful young men, mown down in
their stately prime, became too much for me. I forgot the great ideas to sympathize with the poor
mothers, who had nursed their precious forms, only
to see them all lopped and gashed." For the first time,

she was alienated in spirit from Mazzini; as the dreadful battle proceeded she saw less and less of him. A letter from Rebecca Spring, who was a Quaker pacifist, moved her to write a half-hearted defense of Mazzini's course, but she could not keep up her martial spirit to the end. "Yet the agonies of that baptism of blood, I feel, oh, how deeply! In the golden June days of Rome, consistent in no way, I felt I should have shrunk back—I could not have had it shed."

Meanwhile her letters to the *Tribune* gave a spirited narrative of events. Her description of the demonstration on the Quirinal which preceded the Pope's flight to Gaeta is a typical example of her vigorous pictures. "I returned to the house, which is near the Quirinal. On one side, I could see the palace and gardens of the Pope, on the other the Piazza Barberini and street of the Four Fountains. Presently I saw the carriage of Prince Barberini drive hurriedly into his courtyard gate, the footman signing to close it, a discharge of firearms was heard, and the drums of the Civic Guard beat to arms.

"The padrona ran up and down, crying with every round of shot, 'Jesu Maria, they are killing the Pope! O poor Holy Father!—Tito, Tito,' (out of the window to her husband), 'what *is* the matter?'

"The lord of creation disdained to reply.

" ' O Signora! pray, pray, ask Tito what is the matter?'

" I did so.

" ' I don't know, Signora; nobody knows.'

" ' Why don't you go on the mount and see?'

" ' It would be an imprudence, Signora; nobody will go.'

" I was just thinking to go myself, when I saw a poor man borne by, badly wounded, and heard that the Swiss were firing on the people."

On the 9th of February, 1849, at one o'clock in the morning the Republic was proclaimed, to the ringing of all the bells of Rome. Margaret did not idealize the situation but grasped its sordid realities. " Early next morning I rose and went forth to observe the Republic. Over the Quirinal I went, through the Forum, to the Capitol. There was nothing to be seen except the magnificent calm emperor, the tamers of horses, the fountain, the trophies, the lions, as usual; among the marbles, for living figures, a few dirty, bold women, and Murillo boys in the sun just as usual. I passed into the Corso; there were men in the liberty-caps,—of course the lowest and vilest had been the first to assume it; all the horrible beggars persecuting as impudently as usual." Then she went to hear Mazzini address the Assembly. " He said, ' We will conquer;' whether Rome will, this time, is not to me certain, but such men as Mazzini conquer always, conquer in defeat." She believed in the march of the republic through Europe and prophesied it in these words: "The struggle is now fairly thoroughly commenced, between the principle of democracy and the old powers, no longer legitimate. That struggle may last fifty years, and the earth be watered with the blood and tears of more than one generation, but the result is sure. All Europe, including Great Britain, where the most bitter resistance of all will be made, is to be under republican government in the next century."

It fell to her share to counteract the propaganda stories about anarchy and disorder in Rome. As the interventionists closed in on the republic, these "fe, fo, fum stories", as she called them, multiplied. Indignantly, she declared how she, a woman, alone and unprotected, went about from one end of Rome to the other with perfect security and that her friends sent out their little children with nurses as usual. Never had there been so little crime,—"never was Rome so truly tranquil, so nearly free from gross ill, as this winter." She exposed the methods by which the Oscurantists and interventionists sought to promote riots and disorder. For example, men who appeared in the street and attracted a crowd by behaving as if they were famishing, were arrested by the Civic

Guard and proved to be well-paid agents. A ridiculous story which appeared in foreign newspapers to the effect that red flags were on all the Roman houses as a sign that the Romans were athirst for blood drew forth a humorous protest,—" These flags are put up at the entrance of those streets where there is no barricade as a signal to coachmen and horsemen that they may pass freely. There is one on the house where I am, in which is no person but myself, who thirst for peace, and the Padrone, who thirsts for money."

Her description of the excellent morale of the poor people under the humane influence of the republic was keyed to their own psychology: " Yes, it is true, they cry; . . . we ought not to lie; we should not try to impose upon one another. We ought rather to prefer that our children should work honestly for their bread, than get it by cheating, begging, or the prostitution of their mothers. It would be better to act worthily and kindly, probably would please God more than the kissing of relics. We have long darkly felt these things were so, *now* we know it." Yet her keen observation and honest judgment would not permit her to pass over in silence the " mob of Rome," the " unheeding cabbage-sellers, who never had a thought before beyond contriving how to satisfy their animal instincts for the day."

Without much hope, perhaps, she tried to induce her country to recognize the Roman republic. Republics were few in those days,—she thought they should hang together. " Some of the lowest people have asked me," she wrote, " ' Is it not true that your country had a war to become free? '—' Yes.'—' Then why do they not feel for us? ' " She stated the case for recognition in straightforward American terms. " The suffrage has been correct here, the proportion of votes to the whole population was much larger . . . than it is in our own country at the time of contested elections. . . . If any misrepresentations have induced America to believe, as France affects to have believed, that so large a vote could have been obtained by moral intimidation, the present unanimity of the population in resisting such immense odds, and the enthusiasm of their every expression in favor of the present government, puts the matter beyond a doubt. . . . Since this is the case, surely our country, if no other, is bound to recognize the present government *so long as it can sustain itself.*" But the attitude of the nations was just the opposite. The best blood of Rome, she said bitterly, would " run along the stones, without one nation in the world to defend, one to aid,—scarce one to cry out a tardy ' Shame '! We will wait, whisper the nations, and see if they can bear it. Rack them well to see if they are brave. *If they can do without us,* we will help them."

The surrender came to her at last as a relief from the bloodshed which had grown intolerable. On Monday evening, July 2, she learned that the French were preparing to cross the river and take possession of the city. " I went into the Corso with some friends," she writes. " The lancers of Garibaldi galloped along in full career. . . . We followed them to the piazza of St. John Lateran. . . . The sun was setting, the crescent moon rising, the flower of the Italian youth were marshaling in that solemn place. . . . They had all put on the beautiful dress of the Garibaldi legion, the tunic of bright red cloth, the Greek cap, or else round hat with Puritan plume. Their long hair was blown back from resolute faces; all looked full of courage. . . . They had weighed life and all its material advantages against liberty, and made their election. . . . I saw the wounded, all that could go, laden upon their baggage cars. . . . The women were ready; their eyes were resolved, if sad. The wife of Garibaldi followed him on horseback. He himself was distinguished by the white tunic. . . . He went upon the parapet, and looked upon the road with a spy-glass, and, no obstruction being in sight, he turned his face for a moment back upon Rome, then led the way through the gate. Hard was the heart, stony and seared the eye, that had no tear for that moment. . . . And Rome, anew the Niobe! Must she lose also these beautiful and brave, that promised her regeneration, and would have given it, but for the perfidy, the overpowering force, of the foreign intervention?"

On the morning of July 4, the French troops entered Rome. The population remained indoors with windows closed; whenever a French officer or soldier entered a café, the Italians silently rose and went out. "In two days of French 'order '," Margaret wrote, "more acts of violence have been committed than in two months under the Triumvirate."

Mazzini was still in Rome, and stubbornly refused to leave the city. He walked about the streets, exposing himself to arrest by the French. But for some reason they dared not seize him. Margaret Fuller had not seen him during the last two weeks of the siege. Now she went to search for him and found him in the apartment of Gustavo Modena, the actor. "In two short months," she writes, "he had grown old; all the vital juices seemed exhausted; his eyes were all blood-shot; his skin orange; flesh he had none; his hair was mixed with white; his hand was painful to the touch; but he had never flinched, never quailed; had protested in the last hour against surrender; sweet and calm, but full of a more fiery purpose than ever; in him I revered the hero, and owned myself not of that mold."

It was Margaret Fuller and Giulia Modena who at last persuaded him to leave Rome, and it was Jane Carlyle received and comforted him when he went back to London.

After Mazzini was safe, Margaret remained another day in Rome and went over the scene of the conflict. She saw with her own eyes the awful inequalities of the combat, the superior numbers and organization of the French against the sheer valor of the Italians. Her beloved Italy had been doomed, not at the end when Garibaldi decided on surrender and Mazzini resisted it, but from the very first. " A Contadini showed me where thirty-seven braves are buried beneath a heap of wall that fell upon them in the shock of one cannonade. A marble nymph with broken arm looked sadly that way from her sun-dried fountain; some roses were blooming still, some red oleanders, amid the ruin. . . . This was in the Vascello. I then entered the French ground, all mapped and hollowed like a honeycomb. A pair of skeleton legs protruded from a bank of one barricade; lower, a dog had scratched away its light covering of earth from the body of a man, and discovered it lying face upward all dressed; the dog stood gazing on it with an air of stupid amazement."

CHAPTER XI

1850

ON the day when the French entered Rome, Margaret and Ossoli sat in her chamber and refused to look out of the window. The Roman husband was weeping. They had lost everything; they were empty-handed indeed. "Private hopes of mine are fallen with the hopes of Italy," Margaret wrote; "I have played for a new stake, and lost it."

She went to the American ambassador and begged him to get horses for her, that she might post immediately to Rieti. On arriving there, she found the ten-months-old Nino in such a sad condition of malnutrition that it seemed to her impossible that he could live. The nurse's milk had failed and she had fed the infant on bread and wine. Margaret could only believe that this was a deliberate betrayal of her trust, though the woman had probably but followed the dictates of her own ignorance. At any rate the child had wasted away to nothing and was too weak to lift his hand. He had all but succumbed to a combination of untoward circumstances which Margaret to me silly for a radical like me to be carrying a title; and yet, while Ossoli is in his native land, it seems disjoining myself from him not to bear it. It is a sort of thing that does not naturally belong to me, and, unsustained by fortune, is but a souvenir even for Ossoli. Yet . . . for him to drop an inherited title would be, in some sort, to acquiesce in his brothers' disclaiming him, and to abandon a right he may passively wish to maintain for his child. . . . If Ossoli should drop the title, it would be a suitable moment to do so on becoming an inhabitant of Republican America." All of which sounds very sensible and sincere and not at all " snobbish " and bedazzled.

The Ossolis lived in Florence from October until the following June,—no doubt incurring a debt by doing so. They had a little apartment overlooking the Piazza Santa Maria Novella. There was a grate-fire in the sitting-room and a Roman lamp on the table, beside which Margaret and her husband sat reading in the evening. Their only luxuries were their principles. While the Austrians paraded and beat their drums in the Piazza below, Ossoli wore the uniform of the defeated within doors,—the brown and red coat of the Civic Guard. He and Margaret were greatly depressed by the atmosphere of reaction in which Florence was submerged. Their ardent republicanism, their affection for the child, and their mutual love were the strong bonds between them. When they went out, they frequently went their separate ways: Ossoli, to his vesper services and cafés and Margaret to the society of English and American friends.

The Brownings were in Florence and Margaret met them there for the first time. Mrs. Browning's child was several months younger than Margaret's. The meeting between the two middle-aged mothers piques the imagination. What did they think of each other? What did Mrs. Browning say about Margaret and Margaret's motherhood in that paper which she afterwards wrote and which was so unaccountably lost? We only know that the Brownings, like everyone else, were impressed by Margaret's brilliant powers of conversation, and wondered at the comparatively poor account of her mind and personality given by her writings.

During her winter in Florence, Margaret completed her history of the Roman Revolution. Mrs. Browning said, " It would have been more equal to her faculties than anything she had ever yet produced." There is every reason for believing this to be true. Here she was in her favorite field of politics; she had herself taken part in the secret work of preparation and had shared the counsels of the leaders. In Rome, Ossoli had gleaned for her the news of the cafés daily;

which subsequent and more impressive histories have failed to stress. This was his zeal for the republican form of government. It has come about that the history of Italian unity and Mazzini's place in it has been interpreted by English liberal writers. These historians have usually represented the point of view that a constitutional monarchy does not essentially differ from a republic. As a matter of fact, Mazzini's republicanism was a vital part of his political philosophy; he saw in the spread of republics an essential step toward the United States of Europe, to which he already looked forward. It was natural that Margaret Fuller, as her father's daughter and the pupil of Thomas Jefferson, should understand Mazzini's passion for republics and his ardent belief in their necessity. Her hereditary sympathies were on that side, and she must have seen the practical significance of the leader's republican convictions.

Her book was completed in the spring of 1850, and Margaret made preparations to return to America and find a publisher. It may not be amiss to refer here to Hawthorne's amazing statement that the lamented history (lost with Margaret at sea) never existed at all. Since this opinion is contained in a standard biography and a familiar " reference " work, it cannot be overlooked. But enough has already been said concerning Hawthorne's hysterical prejudice against

Margaret to explain this final fantasy of his unhappy hatred, so that we need not take it too seriously.

When Margaret made her plans for returning to America, she chose perforce the cheapest way of traveling, a sailing vessel from Leghorn to New York loaded with rags and marble. As the journey would last two months, she took a white goat on board to supply Angelino with milk. A young Italian girl named Celesta Pardena, who was on her way to domestic service in America, was engaged to help take care of the baby during the voyage. Horace Sumner of Boston, who had adored Margaret since his student days at Brook Farm and who had spent the winter in Florence in order to be near her, was also of the party. He and Ossoli planned to exchange English and Italian lessons during the voyage. The prospects of the trip, with all its economies, was not unpleasing.

Yet Margaret set sail in a mood of the utmost depression and foreboding. " It has long seemed, that, in the year 1850, I should stand on a plateau in the ascent of life, where I should be allowed to pause for a while, and take more clear and commanding views than ever before. Yet my life proceeds as regularly as the fates of a Greek tragedy, and I can but accept the pages as they turn." In view of what actually happened, her letters written on the eve of the voyage

ners flying; the stern pillar of Hercules all bathed in
roseate vapor; the little white sails diving into the blue
depths with that solemn spoil of the good man, when
he had been so agonized and gasping as the last sun
stooped."

In this letter, mailed at Gibraltar, she told how she
had carried her baby into the sick man's room before
they knew the nature of his disease and feared now
for the child's life. "It is vain by prudence to seek
to evade the stern assaults of destiny. I submit."
This mood of acquiescence was coming to be a per-
sistent one.

After a week in quarantine, the vessel proceeded
under the command of the mate. The fatalities of the
remainder of the voyage have been often related.
Margaret's child succumbed to the smallpox as she
had feared and for days his life was despaired of.
But he recovered at last, and for a brief interval mis-
fortune stayed its hand. Then came the last act of
the tragedy, the shipwreck of the *Elizabeth* just as
she was about to enter the port of New York.

On the eve of landing, a strong gale arose. The
inexperienced mate lost his bearings and the ship
was driven on a sand-bar off Fire Island. The Carrara
marble in the hold completed the wreck. The vessel
at once began to break up but remained afloat ten
hours,—from three o'clock in the morning until one

in the afternoon. A howling gale continued all the while and mountainous seas whipped and tortured the groaning vessel. When the final crash came, Margaret and her husband went down with the ship and their bodies disappeared and were never recovered. The body of Margaret's child was washed up naked on the sands, and was later taken to Mt. Auburn by relatives and buried beside his New England grandfather. The manuscript of her book on the Roman revolution vanished without a trace.

The news of the tragedy sent a shock of horror through the literary world of that day. In the midst of the lamentations and eulogies, Margaret's friends were outraged by the attitude of the mate of the *Elizabeth*. He said that the tragedy was Margaret's own fault. But this was disposed of as an effort in his own defense, because he had left the ship while his passengers were still on board. But the accounts of all the other survivors show that he had grounds for his statement. In one particular their stories all agreed, and this was that Margaret had exerted almost no effort from the beginning to the end to save herself and her family. Her behavior gave the impression of acquiescence in her fate.

The shipwreck was near the shore. According to Bayard Taylor, who went down to survey the scene, the vessel was not more than fifty yards distant from

When the steward, who had remained aboard, saw that the main mast was about to fall, he seized the child, almost by main force, from Margaret's grasp and plunged into the sea with it. Their dead bodies were washed upon the beach soon afterwards, still warm. Ossoli and Celesta clung for a moment at the rigging and then went down together. Margaret went down alone.

Many years before she had once written, "If all the wrecked submitted to be drowned, the world would be a desert." This is a literal description of how she ultimately met her death. She "submitted to be drowned." Her death had in it the elements of pagan acquiescence, of consenting to her destiny.

By a strange coincidence of mischances, no records of her foreign life survived. A trunk, which was washed upon the beach, contained Margaret's correspondence with Ossoli, in Italian, during her stay in Rieti. Beyond this, practically nothing remained.

Within a year or so, a memorial volume was projected by Margaret's New England friends. Giuseppe Mazzini and Mr. and Mrs. Browning were invited to contribute. Carlyle wrote to Emerson, "Browning spoke a long while to me, with emphasis, on the subject [Margaret and her d'Ossoli] . . . I said he ought to send these reminiscences to America; . . .

his answer gave me the impression there had been hindrance somewhere." What could the hindrance have been? At any rate, it was surmounted and both Robert Browning and Elizabeth Browning wrote out their reminiscences of Margaret as they had known her in Florence and sent them to America. They repeatedly assured everyone who asked them about it afterwards that they did write. But the papers never came to light. They were mysteriously lost and no explanation of the loss was ever forthcoming. Furthermore, Mazzini's reminiscences, which he also wrote and sent to America, unaccountably disappeared. Like the Brownings, he afterwards assured inquirers that he had sent a contribution for the Memoirs to America. With one accord, these interesting manuscripts all went astray in the mail. The coincidence strains our credulity. Is it not more likely that an unknown censor interfered? It seems very probable that Mazzini and the Brownings might have written of Margaret's life in Italy with a frankness which did not accord with American standards. What Browning might have said, emphatically, of Margaret and her d'Ossoli; what Mrs. Browning might have spoken of Margaret and her Nino; what Mazzini might have written of Margaret in Rome—over all this one can now only speculate. From comprehending witnesses like these, something significant might well be expected, glimpses of the kind of woman Margaret really was, revelations through the impression she made on personalities with the large tolerance of life which belongs to genius.

It was by her personality rather than her work that she impressed herself on her generation. But the conquest of a personality by a woman and a daughter of Puritanism was a heroic achievement. It meant the overthrow of respectabilities and sacrosanctities on every hand and a degree of resolution which is not supposed to reside in a truly feminine nature.

There were strange contradictions in her life which were a puzzle to her age. Her inconsistencies of health and fluctuations of energy were baffling to those who knew her best. Though always an invalid, she did the work of three women and sometimes " worked better when she was ill." She gave an impression of abundant vitality and a vast fund of energy. Yet there were moments when her energy strangely forsook her, as when she gave herself up without a struggle to the waves. These things were manifestations of hysteria, and Margaret had long been known to have had a neurotic constitution. According to the Freudian psychology, the source of her hysteria was a secret which she kept from herself, from her own consciousness. " Nature keeps so many secrets," she once said, referring to the concealment of her marriage, "that I had supposed the moral writers exaggerated the dangers and plagues of keeping them; but they cannot exaggerate." But the dangers and plagues are greatly enhanced when this conflict with society becomes a conflict within one's own mental life. As Margaret kept the date of her marriage a secret to evade the social censor, she had in earliest childhood undertaken a far more dangerous concealment, the concealment from the inward censor of an erotic element in her love for a deeply reverenced father. Yet with her whole conscious nature, Margaret loved the truth and never ceased from following it. "I feel the strength to dispense with all illusions," she said; "I will stand ready and rejoice in the severest probations." In this kind of ordeal she was profoundly courageous.

She took for her chief interests in life two subjects which were in her day regarded as outside of woman's sphere. Her favorite themes were love and politics. Nowadays she would be permitted to take an interest in politics but she would still find that love was for her sex a forbidden topic.

The general cast of her political views was determined far back in her childish years, when Timothy Fuller had ripped out sarcasms against the Allies who had put down Jacobinism in France and restored Bourbonism instead. Margaret's mind received then a permanent impression, which caused her to stand, thirty years later, as she did, with the forces of young Italy against papal Bourbonists of Rome.

She was a passionate advocate of economic reforms and women's rights. For women also, she held, the career should be open to talent. " Another century," she wrote, " and I might ask to be made Ambassador myself,—'tis true, like other Ambassadors, I would employ clerks to do most of the duty." Indeed, Margaret would have made an excellent ambassador. One who unites the ability to appreciate Tasso manuscripts with the power to tame Garibaldi's Legionaries is not found for the Italian embassy every day.

In the psychology of love, she was a pioneer. Though it is considered womanly to love and un-womanly not to love, to take an intelligent and out-spoken interest in the subject is quite another matter. A woman should open her mouth and shut her eyes. Margaret had too much curiostiy, too much veracity, and too little naïveté to please the ideas of the parochial society in which she lived. Even liberal-minded Transcendentalists who regarded the devil as a superstition, believed in the existence of the " baser instincts " and the extirpation of the " lower impulses " by the higher will-power.

To Margaret's way of thinking, confirmed and strengthened by the influence of Goethe, the vast separation between good and evil impulses in human nature was not so clear. Neither did she believe that the baser instincts could be refined away through a series of easy victories, although she was anything but a materialist in her conception of love. She believed in the hunger of the affections, because she had experienced it. "Imperfect as love is," she wrote in the last year of her life, " I want human beings to love, as I suffocate without." Though she did not generalize from her experience, she did acknowledge the fulfilment of the law in her own case and thereby set an example of admitting the emotional necessities of life.

Her biographers often speak of this characteristic of Margaret's nature as if it were the exceptional trait of her unusual disposition. As a matter of fact, it is a universal trait of normal human nature, and Margaret's originality lay in the frank admission of it. Acknowledging her debt to nature, she had the good sense to pay as she could, and, to use her own words, "not calculate too closely ". Her life was a vindication of her belief, as an intellectual woman, in the reality of the instinctive life; as it was also a vindication of her belief, as an instinctive woman, in the reality of the intellectual life.

BIBLIOGRAPHY

LITERARY WORKS OF MARGARET FULLER OSSOLI

In the order of their production

Eckermann's Conversations with Goethe. Translation. Specimens of Foreign Standard Literature, Vol. IV. Boston, Hilliard, Gray and Co., 1839.

Correspondence of Fräulein Günderode and Bettina von Arnim. Joint translation with Minna Wesselhoeft. Boston, Burnham, 1861.

The Dial; a magazine for literature, philosophy, and religion. Edited by Margaret Fuller, R. W. Emerson, and George Ripley. Boston, 1840-1844.

Summer on the Lakes, in 1843. Boston, Little Brown, 1844.

Woman in the Nineteenth Century. Introduction by Horace Greeley. Boston, Jewett, 1855.

Literature and Art: Essays. Introduction by Horace Greeley. New York, Fowler and Wells, 1852.

Life Without and Life Within: Essays. New York, Tribune Association, 1869.

Love Letters, 1845-1846. Introduction by Julia Ward Howe. New York, Appleton, 1903.

At Home and Abroad, or, Things and Thoughts in America and Europe. New York, Tribune Association, 1869.

BIOGRAPHICAL SOURCES.

Caroline W. Dall. *Historical Pictures: Margaret Fuller.* Boston, Lee and Shepard, 1860.

R. W. Emerson, W. H. Channing, and J. F. Clarke. *Memoirs of Margaret Fuller Ossoli.* New York, Tribune Association, 1869.

Thomas Wentworth Higginson. *Margaret Fuller Ossoli.* Boston, Houghton Mifflin, 1884.

Thomas Wentworth Higginson. Margaret Fuller, in *Eminent Women of the Age.* Hartford, Betts, 1869.

Julia Ward Howe. *Margaret Fuller (Marquesa Ossoli).* Boston, Roberts, 1883.

Andrew Macphail. Margaret Fuller, in *Essays in Puritanism.* Boston, Houghton Mifflin, 1905.

PSYCHOLOGICAL SOURCES.

S. Ferenczi. *Contributions to Psychoanalysis.* Boston, Badger, 1916.

217

Sigmund Freud. *Delusion and Dream.* New York, Moffat Yard, 1917.
    The Interpretation of Dreams. New York, Macmillan, 1912.
    Leonardo da Vinci. New York, Moffat Yard, 1916.

Horace Westlake Frink. *Morbid Fears and Compulsions.* New York, Moffat Yard, 1918.

Mary Keyt Isham. *Real Womanliness the Basis of a Career.* New York Times Magazine. November 28, 1915.

Ernest Jones. *Papers on Psychoanalysis.* London, Baillière Tindall, 1913.

C. G. Jung. *Collected Papers on Analytical Psychology.* Edited by Dr. Constance Long. London, Baillière Tindall, 1916.
    Psychology of the Unconscious. Introduction by Beatrice M Hinkle, M.D, New York, Moffat Yard, 1916.

GENERAL SOURCES

John Quincey Adams. *Memoirs.* Philadelphia, Lippincott, 1874-1877.

Matilde Blind. *George Eliot.* Boston, Roberts. 1883

Frederick Augustus Braun. *Margaret Fuller and Goethe.* New York, Holt, 1910.
    Margaret Fuller's Translation and Criticism of Goethe's Faust. *Journal of English and Germanic Philology,* April, 1914.

Fredrika Bremer. *Homes of the New World.* New York, Harper, 1854.

Albert Brisbane. *Social Destiny of Man.* Philadelphia, Stollmeyer, 1840.

Jane Welsh Carlyle. *Letters and Memorials.* New York, Scribner's, 1883.

Thomas Carlyle and Ralph Waldo Emerson. *Correspondence.* Boston, Osgood, 1883.

Richard V. Carpenter. Margaret Fuller in Nothern Illinois. *Journal of the Illinois State Historical Society.* Springfield, January, 1910

G. K. Chesterton. *Robert Browning.* New York, Macmillan, 1903.

Lydia Maria Child. *Memoirs of Mme. de Stael and Mme. Roland.* New York, C. S. Francis, 1847.

J. W. Cross. *George Eliot's Life as Related in her Letters and Journals.* New York, Harper, 1855.

Ralph Waldo Emerson. Historic Notes of Life and Letters in Massachusetts. *Atlantic Monthly,* October, 1883.
    Mary Moody Emerson. *Atlantic Monthly,* December, 1883.

Eliza Ware Farrar. *Recollections of Seventy Years.* Boston, Osgood, 1866.

Margaret Fuller. Letter to E. A. Duyckinck. Manuscript; New York Public Library.

Octavius B. Frothingham. *Transcendentalism in New England.* Boston, American Unitarian Association, 1876.

H. C. Goddard. New England Transcendentalism, in *Cambridge History of American Literature.* New York, Putnam, 1917.

William Godwin. *Memoirs of Mary Wollstonecraft Godwin,* author of "A Vindication of the Rights of Woman." Philadelphia, Carey, 1799.

Horace Greeley. *Recollections of a Busy Life.* New York, Tribune Association, 1869.

Horace Greeley and Robert Dale Owen. Discussion of the Law of Divorce. In *Recollections.* New York, Tribune Association, 1869.

Horace Greeley and H. J. Raymond. *Association Discussed, or the Socialism of the* Tribune *Examined.* New York, Harper, 1847.

Frank Harris. Carlyle, in *Contemporary Portaits.* New York, Kennerley, 1915.

Julian Hawthorne. *Nathaniel Hawthorne and His Wife.* Boston, Osgood, 1885.

Nathaniel Hawthorne. *Blithedale Romance.* Boston, Osgood, 1852.

Morris Hillquit. *History of Socialism in the United States.* New York, Funk and Wagnalls, 1903.

Henry James. *William Wetmore Story and His Friends.* Boston, Houghton Mifflin, 1903.

Bolton King. *History of Italian Unity.* London, Nisbet, 1899. *Mazzini.* New York, Dutton, 1902.

Karl Knortz. *Brook Farm und Margaret Fuller.* New York, Bartsch, 1886.

James Russell Lowell. *Fable for Critics.* New York, Putnam, 1848.

Harriet Martineau. *Autobiography.* Boston, Osgood, 1877. *Society in America.* New York, Harper, 1837.

Giuseppe Mazzini. George Sand, in *Critical Essays.* London, Smith Elder, 1891. *Letters to the Italian Working Class.* London, Smith Elder, 1891.

James Parton. *Life of Horace Greeley.* Boston, Osgood, 1869.

Frank B. Sanborn. *Recollections of Seventy Years.* Boston, Badger, 1909.

L. C. Scott. *Life and Letters of Christopher Pearse Cranch.* Boston, Houghton Mifflin, 1917.

Charles Sotheran. *Horace Greeley and other Pioneers of American Socialism.* New York, Humboldt Publishing Co., 1892.

Elizabeth Cady Stanton and Susan B. Anthony. *History of Woman Suffrage*. New York, Fowler and Wells, and Rochester, Susan B. Anthony. 1881-192.

Frank Preston Stearns. *The Life and Genius of Nathaniel Hawthorne*. Philadelphia, Lippincott, 1906.

George Robert Stirling Taylor. *Mary Wollstonecraft*. New York, John Lane, 1911.

Lilian Whiting. *The Brownings, Their Life and Art*. Boston, Little Brown, 1911.

INDEX